Hiring Contractors

THE NO-HEADACHE APPROACH

Steven VanCauwenbergh
Walter Jenkins

Hiring Contractors
The No-Headache Approach

International Standard Book Number: 978-0-9859805-6-6

Copyright © 2014 by Steven VanCauwenbergh
All rights reserved. No part of this publication may be reproduced, stored in a retrieval system, or transmitted in any form by any means, electronic, mechanical, photocopy, recording, or otherwise, without the prior permission of the author, except as provided for by USA copyright law.

First printing 2014

Printed in the United States of America

Library of Congress Cataloging-in-Publication Data
is available from the publisher

This publication is designed to provide competent and reliable information regarding the subject matter covered for informational purposes. However, it is sold with the understanding that the author and publisher are not engaged in rendering legal, financial, or other professional advice. Laws and practices often vary from state to state and if legal or other expert assistance is required, the services of a professional should be sought. The author and publisher specifically disclaim any liability that is incurred from the use or application of the contents of this book. While every attempt has been made to verify the information in this book, neither the author nor his affiliates/partners assume any responsibility for errors, inaccuracies, or omissions.

**Published by Teflon Publishing,
8 NE 48th Street, Oklahoma City, OK 73105**
The Savvy Landlord name and logo are trademarks of Teflon Publishing
Library of Congress Cataloging-in-Publication data
is available from the publisher

Interior design by Thomas White with Imprint Media
Cover design by Elizabeth Hunt with Gorilla Media Group
www.gorillamediagroup.com

To my savvy children Kennedy Grace, Maxwell James, and Katy Shay for being true negotiators to get what they want.

-**Love Dad**

CONTENTS

INTRODUCTION 1
THE PROCESS 4
MAKE SURE HE'S NOT FULL OF HOT AIR 11
SWEAT EQUITY 14
    GET YOUR MIND OUT OF THE SEWER 14
    EIGHT BUCKS 18
    COUNTERTOP 20
    ROOF A DUPLEX 22
    COVER YOURSELF 25
    MERRY CHRISTMAS 28
    I FOUND A GOOD GUY 32
    FUN WITH FOUNDATION 37
THE QUEST 42
PUT ME IN, COACH 79
RED FLAGS & SCAMS 81
    RED FLAGS 81
    SCAMS 85
SPOKEN LIKE A PRO 90
BONUS INTERVIEW 146
TEN EMPOWERING TIPS 154
TIME TO ROLL 159
LEARN CONTRACTOR LINGO: TERMINOLOGY 160

INTRODUCTION

Every real estate investor will eventually have to hire a contractor. It is an ugly fact of life. A pipe will burst, an electrical wire will short out, or walls will need to be repainted. And many people don't have the time or skill to do those things themselves. So we have to hire people to do those things for us.

That sounds simple, and it can be when we hire the right people. The right contractor can save you time and money and lower your stress when things go wrong.

But hiring the wrong contractor can make things unbearable. Working with the wrong contractor is like inviting a thief into your home. He steals your money, your time, and your peace of mind and won't leave until there is nothing left to take.

I know because, like every investor I've talked to, I have hired the wrong contractor to work for me. More than once, I have looked at shoddy work that was overpriced and not completed on time. It's frustrating, and it makes me wonder if there are any honest contractors in the world.

Hiring Contractors

Working with a contractor (especially if you own multiple properties) is like a marriage. When everyone is on the same page, it's a great experience. But being pulled in different directions causes pain and can lead to emotional and financial ruin.

My hope is that when you read this book, you will be able to prequalify potential contractors so you don't let the wrong people onto your property. When you are educated, you can overcome fear and be empowered. You will know what to look for and see the red flags as they pop out of a dishonest contractor's mouth.

These tips will be especially helpful for real estate investors as they transition from a few properties to a dozen or more properties. As you build your empire, you won't be able to maintain, repair, and rehab properties by yourself, and you shouldn't try to. You have to rely on contractors to leverage your time. It's the only way to build the security you and your family deserve. With the techniques you will learn in the pages that follow, you will know what to look for and what to avoid, and you can keep the thieves out of your house and in prison where they belong.

This book is broken into sections to help you resolve the issues you will face when you need to hire a contractor. In **Sweat Equity**, I share some of the experiences I have faced. In **The Process**, I detail how I hire contractors. **The Quest** is a list of sixty questions and answers you should know when dealing with contractors. They cover some of the most common issues property owners face when they hire someone to work

Introduction

on a house or apartment. **Spoken Like a Pro** contains interviews from real estate investors who have hired numerous contractors, and it also shares secrets from a professional contractor. At the back of the book I have included a glossary with definitions of some of the most common terms contractors use, and it discloses some of the most frequent scams in the contracting world.

Like the other books in The Savvy Landlord series, this book is a powerful tool that will cut the learning curve you will face as you build your empire. Happy reading, and may your next deal be your best deal.

THE PROCESS

Hiring a contractor isn't as simple as pulling a name off of the Internet and writing a check. Before you need to hire someone, have a process in place. This ensures you won't make a huge mistake if you have to call a plumber at 3:00 a.m. because you have a busted pipe in an occupied property. When I have a specific job I need to tackle, I try to have a general idea of what type of contractor I am looking for. Does the job require unskilled labor or skilled labor?

Unskilled labor is perfect for picking stuff up after a job, moving trash, landscaping, or even simple painting jobs. Never pay for skilled labor when unskilled labor will get the job done. Overpaying contractors will kill your cash flow.

After I know what kind of labor I need, I ask a few questions. What is it worth in terms of time and resources to get the job done? How long is it going to take and when do I need it done? If I have a house that's empty, my job is to get the work done and rent the property as soon as possible. I'm looking to have the best work done as fast as possible at the best price.

The Process

When I need a new roof, the first thing I do is get a general idea of what roofing material is going to cost. I'm also going to familiarize myself with the terminology so that when I communicate with a contractor, I know exactly what he is saying. If I speak the roofer's language, I seem educated as opposed to some ignorant person who's going to pay the most because he doesn't know what is going on and can't ask the right questions.

Roofers speak in terms of squares. That's how they measure roofs and calculate the amount of material they need. A square is 100 square feet, which is a ten-by-ten space. When the contractor jumps on the roof and says, "You are going to need twenty-four squares," I check with a local supply house and find out how much the material will cost.

Arm yourself with as much information as possible so you can make sound decisions. I get three bids if possible, but I also try to work with the same contractor. There's one I've had great success with, and I'll wait until he is available to get the job done because I know his skill set and the quality of his work.

When contractors come out to give you bids, ask as many questions as you can. You will learn something different from their answers. You're not just looking for the answer. You want to test them to make sure they are genuine and have the skill level you are looking for. Ask them about jobs they have done and drive by and see them. Make sure their work passes the eye test. Call the investor or property owner and ask a few questions: Did you like them? Did they clean up when the work was complete? Did they pick up all the nails on the ground? These are the questions you need to ask about every contractor.

If you ask a contractor how he is going to replace a roof, he might say, "Well, we have to remove the shingles. I need to bring a trailer. I drop the material off or have it delivered."

Ask as many questions as you need to feel comfortable. It's your responsibility and your money. You are the one paying for it, and you need to think about every detail of every job that is done on your properties.

When you are talking to contractors and they are explaining step-by-step on how they are going to tear your roof off and put a new one on, you will hear clues about the important parts of the job. One contractor may tell you he prefers fifteen-pound felt and another may say he likes thirty-pound felt. When that happens, ask, "Why? What do you recommend?"

I ask every contractor I work with, "Do you guarantee your work?" and then I give him a possible repair scenario. "What happens if it leaks? How do I handle that? Are you going to come right over, and will you charge me a fee?" I want to hear the answer, but I also watch facial expressions when I ask about warranty work. Most people have a pretty good sense of when someone is lying to them, and if your contractor gives off bad vibes look for someone else.

Due diligence always pays off. Know what you are looking for and you can separate the professional contractors from the professional conmen. You have to interview people, do some searching, and use tools such as Google and YouTube to be empowered and make the best decision.

SPARKY

When you need to hire an electrician, always look for skilled contractors. Don't take these situations lightly. If someone doesn't know what he is doing and grabs onto one of the power lines on your property, things can turn dangerous in a heartbeat.

I don't always hire licensed individuals. I might get an unlicensed (but skilled) individual to switch out some outlets, put in a 220 dryer line, an electrical outlet, or a GFI outlet.

A few years ago, I purchased a property that had been vacant for over ten years, and our local electrical utility company removed the line from their main supply to the house. There was no electricity on the property.

The first thing I had to do was figure out how much it was going to cost to get power on the property and what the process of getting it done would entail. I had to understand the scope of it.

I would normally call an electrician who would come over and handle everything. He would give me a bid that included the permits and the inspections.

Hiring Contractors

To see if he is the right man for the job, I would ask him, "Where have you worked? How long have you been in business?" If you ask the right questions in a relaxed manner, they will spill the beans. They might say "I just got out of jail," or "I've been a journeyman for the last five years," or "I worked for another company for five years but I'm on my own now." His answers and how he answers will give me all the information I need.

I ask more questions after he submits his bid, such as, "How did you come up with this price so I can get this approved through my partner?"

I always mention a partner. However, that partner can mean my dog, my daughter, or my friend. This gives me a way out if they keep calling and asking me, "Am I going to get the job?" or "When can we start?" I can always say, "I haven't heard back from my partner," or "My partner already has decided to go somewhere else and use another electrician. Sorry."

It takes the pressure off of me and I don't have to be the bad guy. I may need this electrician on another job, and if he's frustrated because he drove to a job site in 100-degree weather but didn't get hired he may not be there when I need him down the line.

Contractors are human. You need to treat them with respect and speak their language. I always try to come across as a blue-collar individual. I know what it takes to be self-employed because I am self-employed. I try to meet contractors on common ground, and I don't act like a big bad landlord with hundreds of properties. I would never say, "You need to give me a discount or I'm going to call someone else." I respect them and understand their skill level is different from my skill level. My skill level is how to find properties and purchase them and their skill level is to wire them, replace the roofs on them, or fix broken plumbing.

You have to learn to make sound decisions. Sometimes, you have to go with your gut. I have paid $600 to replace a breaker box, and I have spent $1,200 for the same work. The price depends on the situation and my needs. The $1,200 breaker box came after a storm and I needed it to be done ASAP. The guy took me for a ride because he knew I was in a bind. I should also tell you I have used someone else on a different job and got it done for $600 because he was desperate and needed work. Using leverage to adjust the price works both ways. I've hired a guy I trusted to do this same work who charged me $1,000. He may not have had the lowest bid, but he's done several jobs for me so I knew that he would do it right and be thorough.

One of the most frustrating things you will encounter is when a contractor who only cares about getting a quick payday and is only concerned with one area when other areas need to be addressed. I have come to appreciate contractors who take care of everything and get the job done thoroughly before they leave the site. They want to do the job once and to do it right, even if that means talking to me about things I didn't mention when I contacted them. I know they are not trying to upsell me. They are trying to help me.

Hiring the right contractor will change the way you do business and help you grow your empire. It's another set of eyes to inspect and work on your houses each and every day. You won't have to climb on roofs or through attics, so it's a huge advantage to have a relationship with a contractor you trust.

When your project requires permits or inspections, do not pay the contractor until the inspector signs off on it. If it doesn't pass inspection, don't pay until any problems are corrected. I once made the mistake of paying before an inspection was done. I had to hire someone else to pull another permit and get the property ready for inspection. It caused a lot of stress, and I don't want you to go through that. Be savvy. Learn from my mistake and keep your money safe.

I have said this before, but I can't stress it enough. Hopefully, you will hear these words in your dreams. *Never pay a contractor until you're completely satisfied with his work.* Once you sign the check, you may never see him again. Don't say I didn't warn you.

MAKE SURE HE'S NOT FULL OF HOT AIR

At some point, you will have to hire someone to work on your heating or air conditioning. Hiring a HVAC (heating, ventilation, and air conditioning) contractor always requires extremely skilled labor. It will probably be the most expensive repair or installation you will undertake while rehabbing, remodeling, or maintaining property as an investor, and you have to be extremely careful when choosing this type of contractor.

When I hire a heat and air contractor, I have a series of thoughts and questions. What am I getting into? How long is the repair/installation going to take? How expensive is it going to be, what's my end result, and when can I get it done? HVAC prices are all over the map. This is true with a lot of contracting jobs, but HVAC seems to be the worst. It's not uncommon for HVAC bids to vary by as much as $2,000.

There are many reasons for this. Heating and air businesses are extremely busy during the summer. There are more service calls and more repairs when the weather is hot because most people run their cooling systems nonstop. HVAC contractors may even be weeks behind in the peak season. They may refuse to take small jobs or those they don't think are worth their time.

How can you use this to your advantage as an investor? I like purchasing property in the fall and winter because most heat and air guys are hungry for work during that time, and they're willing to take a discounted rate just to have the business. They have expenses, and they have salaries to pay. If you time it right, you can use that to save you money.

Don't try to save money by hiring unlicensed HVAC contractors. I have been burned several times when I hired people who were in the process of getting their licenses, who were journeymen, or were apprentices. They knew their stuff and I thought they did good work, but it cost me in the long run.

I built a relationship with one of these individuals and I trusted his skill level and felt he could do anything. He had installed brand-new units for three years as an apprentice.

He opened his own company, and he would do a service call for $50 or less. "This is great," I thought. He had his EPA license, so he could purchase Freon and service my air conditioners. After a few months, his invoices started getting higher and higher. Those great discounts soon disappeared. I got lazy and he started charging me what a licensed contractor would. If you hire someone who's unlicensed, you should pay a substantially discounted rate. It felt like a slap in the face when I figured out I was paying him as much as a licensed HVAC guy.

Make Sure He's Not Full Of Hot Air

If I'm going to pay the amount a licensed contractor would charge, I'm going to go with a reputable company that's going to warranty its work, that wants my business, that has insurance, that has a billing department, and that can (and will) return my phone calls in a timely manner.

I learned my lesson the hard way. If you're dealing with a highly skilled, licensed contractor, it's going to cost you 10, 20, or maybe even 30 percent more, but it's worth the expense, and you're going to sleep better at night. If you have a dispute, an unlicensed individual can easily disappear, but a licensed contractor is more apt to take care of you because he needs to keep his license.

SWEAT EQUITY

"Where success is concerned people are not measured in inches, or pounds, or college degrees, or family background; they are measured by the size of their thinking."

-David Schwartz

GET YOUR MIND OUT OF THE SEWER

One day I got a call from a neighbor who owned a property behind one of my duplexes. He told me sewage was seeping into his backyard. I thought it was no big deal. I called a company I use to take care of things like that. They came out, pumped it, and everything was great. I paid their $200 bill and thought the sewage problem was over.

About a week later, the neighbor called me again and said the sewage was still seeping out. I told him, "That can't be true. I just paid for that." I didn't know what was happening. I called the company back and they sent a crew out again. They told me my septic tank needed to be replaced.

I was shocked and frustrated. I had never done that before and didn't know how much it would cost. I had a septic tank contractor come out and explain the situation to me. He told me there are a bunch of laws and Department of Environmental Quality (DEQ) regulations and drama about installing a new septic tank. "You have a water well right here," he said. "You can't stick a septic tank that close to a well. Plus, your property line ends and your septic tank is in someone else's backyard. And before we can do anything, you have to have a soil test."

Before I could do any work, I had to purchase the land or convince the landowner behind me to let me repair or replace a septic tank on his property. I was over a barrel and I didn't know what to do. The work was going to cost $6,000 to $12,000, but it had to be done.

My first hurdle was to get the landowner behind my property to give me permission to work on his land. I called my local title company and explained the situation. They helped me and drew up an easement agreement, which I took to the landowner. He understood and was willing to help as long as it meant sewage would stop spewing all over his yard.

Then I moved on to the next item on my list. I paid $200 for a soil test, and that determined what type of septic tank I could install. There are two main types of septic tanks, aerobic systems and lateral line systems. A lateral line system is low maintenance and basically takes care of itself.

An aerobic system is a giant headache that can have electricity issues. It has several different chambers, and there are certain things you can't put down the drain. Once the soil test was done, the contractor told me, "We can do a lateral line system. We have to rip everything out, but it can be done. It's going to cost $10,000." Saying that didn't faze him one bit because he wasn't the one writing the check.

I was stuck. I had already spent two weeks getting permission. "Go ahead. Let's get it done." But I had to wait because I didn't have the money. I was waiting for the first of the month when my rent checks started rolling in. To make matters worse, I had to ask the contractor to inspect a septic tank on another property two blocks away. Sewage was spilling out all over that lawn as well. I was getting tickets from the city, and it was paramount that I get the tank repairedreplaced immediately, even though it was going to cost another $6,000.

That lucky contractor got to install two septic tanks for one customer. I had to go through the same process on the second property. I had to get a soil test. I had to get information from the DEQ and so on and so forth. I jumped through all those hoops and was ready to install the first tank at the beginning of the month and the second one the following month.

I was excited until tenants started calling me. They couldn't use the facilities because the sewer was backing up. The neighbors were complaining and they got the city involved. I told the contractor how important it was that we get the work done at the first of the month and he assured me it would be done.

Everything was in place and I told the tenants we were good to go. They were fine. I called the contractor to confirm the work and he told me, "I'm real busy right now. I can't get to it until the following month."

Things started unraveling after that, and problems started popping up.

One was that he was charging me a fee to pump out the tank. I thought, "Shouldn't that be included in the price?"

When the start date rolled around, I texted the tenant and asked, "Are the crews there? I'm ready to come over there and inspect it so I can pay the contractor." The tenant texted back, "We haven't seen them." I called the contractor and said, "Where are you?"

"We're behind because of a storm. It's going to be another two weeks."

I was ticked and let the contractor know it. "That's not going to work. I promised the city that we're going to take care of it as soon as possible. You're making this whole situation worse than it already is. It's becoming a lot of pressure." The guy started yelling and going off on me.

I was getting wise at his game and called other septic tank contractors. Another contractor promised to get over there in a week. He got over there and did the job as he promised. I was shocked because I had endured this two-month ordeal and another contractor was able get it done in a single day.

Before I hired the new contractor, I sent a fax to the old contractor and said, "We're no longer going to use your services due to the delays and false promises. We're not going to need your service." The guy called and started cursing at me. He had the nerve to tell me I owed him $250 for consulting and $200 for the permit, and that he was going to put a lien on the property.

I hung up on him and started digging into what he told me. I was really distraught at the thought of him placing a lien on my property. I called the city and discovered he never paid for the permit. That was interesting because I had a invoice from him that stated otherwise. I talked to the second contractor about it, and he told me there was no permit issued on the property other than the one for which he had paid.

Then I checked with a friend who happens to be an attorney. He told me there was no way the contractor could put a lien on my property. That was hot air, like everything else the contractor told me.

The moral of the story is you never know what you're going to get into. I trusted the first contractor. I have no idea why he was delaying me. I was willing to pay for the work, and I didn't negotiate his fees.

Check, verify, do your diligence, and have safeguards in place.

Eight Bucks

Some people say $8 won't get you very much, but I disagree. A few years ago, I rehabbed the largest project of my life. It was a three-story, fourteen-unit apartment complex, and if you read the first Savvy Landlord book, you know it as "The Fourteen-Eyed Monster." I owned that property early in my career when I was a newbie, and I really didn't comprehend the scale of the project. I had to rip out every piece of carpet on three floors, tear down ceilings, and remove walls. It never occurred to me how I was going to haul trash out of that monstrosity.

I had no idea how much the project was going to cost, so I called contractors who specialized in hauling trash out of buildings. They drove over to the apartment, looked around, and gave me bids, which ranged from $1,200 to $3,500, not including the dump fees or the trash container fee. "There has to be a better way," I thought.

I came up with the idea of doing it myself. I had a trash container delivered and decided to put Craigslist to the test. I ran an ad that read, "Need help picking up trash, light painting, and various maintenance jobs. Pays cash, $8 an hour." The ad went ballistic. I could not get to the computer fast enough to pull the ad down. The phone was ringing nonstop. I told the callers where the job was going to be and to show up at 8:00 a.m. the next morning ready to work.

Ten people confirmed over the phone, and four showed up on time. They went to work and emptied the entire building. It was amazing. In fact, they did such a good job I had to tell one of the guys, "Sir, I don't need your services anymore." The three guys who stayed killed it for the whole week. Actually, the entire teardown only took three days. After they were done, I kept one guy, and I used him on several other jobs.

Here's how the math worked out. It took three days total. The first day I hired four guys at $8 an hour for eight hours, and that came to $256. The second day, I dropped a guy, kept three others, and they worked eight hours at $8 an hour. That cost me $192, and I did the same thing on the third day, which was another $192. It cost me $640 to remove all the carpet, all the trash, all the sheet rock, all the debris, and all the wood. I used one container, and that cost $300. My total bill was under $1,000.

Hiring Contractors

I still use Craigslist when I need general laborers, and I have found some good workers. If a guy stays around for a while or does a really good job, I give him a pay bump to $9 an hour to really ramp him up. Then, if he does really well after a few months, I go up to $10 an hour. I keep escalating the hourly rate depending on their skill level, what they get done in a timely manner, and if they're neat and clean.

COUNTERTOP

I purchased a property at a discount and it needed a lot of work, including redoing the flooring and replacing the old windows. I decided to act as my own general contractor and had to start from scratch in every room. I lived on the property while it was being remodeled.

I was getting to the end of the remodeling and still had to do the kitchen, which included replacing an outdated Formica countertop. The neighborhood was upper-middle class, and a lot of the homes were 2,000 to 2,500 square feet or more. The rage at the time was solid epoxy-type countertops. Granite was still popular, but tile was out. HGTV was coming out with concrete countertops. I knew I would eventually sell this property, so I did my research on what type of countertop to install so I would get the most bang for my buck when I sold it.

I decided to go with Corian which is one solid epoxy piece. I called a contractor and she shot me a price of $4,000. I was shocked at the price, but after I thought about it, I understood why it was so much. The countertop was an odd shape and extremely large. It was attached to a bar and a separate island, as well as another area for the stove. The surface area of the counter space was nearly ninety-square-feet.

Because of the cost, I decided to stick with Formica. I called another company, and they came out and gave me a bid. They quoted me $2,200 to replace the top and install a new Formica custom countertop. That was doable. It's not what I wanted, but I had to make a decision to replace the tacky countertop, and Formica was within my budget.

I was about to pull the trigger on the job. I felt confident, and I really trusted the guy. He gave me a lot of information and told me what was going to happen during the process. He told me it was going to smell like glue, and that there was going to be a lot of dust. He said he would use drop cloths to cover everything, but it wouldn't completely protect the rest of the house. He suggested I might not want to be there for a few days. The guy was thorough and I had a good feeling about him. He did such a good job in his sales presentation that I emulated him and tried to use the same techniques in my business.

I called one more contractor and was impressed with him. When we talked, we really connected. He gave me a bid of $1,400, which included tiling the back splash all the way around the kitchen. I was stunned.

The only thing I had to do was buy the travertine tile. In my mind, I was getting a custom countertop for $1,100 and had to pay another $300 for the tile job. In four years, I could replace the countertop again with the newest hip color and still have paid less than I would have for the $4,000

Corian counter. I selected a style of Formica that looked like granite with a unique bull-nose edge. I told the guy to go ahead and do the job.

He came out and did a wonderful job. It took three days, which was longer than expected. The only drawback was a seam over the dishwasher that wasn't secured and had a little bubble in it. There was no way to avoid the seam because they didn't make a single sheet of Formica large enough to cover the bar area of the countertop.

I asked him, "What's up with this?"

"It will relax after a while," he told me and said I shouldn't worry about it. But it never relaxed, and every time I looked at the bubble it drove me crazy.

I have since moved out and a family rents the property now. I don't have to look at that bubble anymore.

I learned a lot from that project. If I had to do it again, I probably wouldn't go with Formica. I would have researched concrete countertops, which might have been the hippest or most economical choice. But I learned my lesson and moved on down the line.

Roof a Duplex

I thought I got an awesome deal on a duplex. I saw the lead at my local REIA and was surprised to see someone trying to sell a duplex for $19,000. I researched the property and the numbers just didn't jive at $19,000. I made a few calls, the wholesaler handed the deal to another wholesaler, and I got it under contract for $11,000. I gave the rookie wholesaler a finder's fee of $500.

The fact that I was able to get the property for such a discounted price should have told me something, but I chalked it up to the fact I am a savvy investor and an all-around great guy. I dove into the project and realized I would have to gut the whole thing out from top to bottom. The first thing I had to tackle was the leaking roof.

I called a roofing contractor who was known in the local real estate group and who warrantied his work in writing. The property had been vacant for at least eleven years, and I knew I was going to come across some major issues. I expected to pay for some repairs. I ran the numbers in my head and budgeted $5,000 for the roof. It was a relatively small duplex, and I thought that would more than cover it.

The roofer came out and gave me a bid of $8,500. I couldn't believe it. "Wow!" What's wrong?"

"There are three layers that need to be removed. It's a shake roof on top of slats, and we have to re-deck it."

I was floored. I thought I had made a great purchase, but now I had to spend almost $9,000 on a roof.

I looked at the roof and there were several areas where it dipped and needed to be shored up. The back of the roof needed to be jacked up. I had a conversation with the contractor, and we were on the same page. We knew we were about to open up a can of worms, and I was fine with that. I factored in the extra costs for the repairs including fascia and soffit work.

He said he had a great a carpenter who could handle anything. He said the carpenter was cheap, which was something I needed to hear. After the roof was torn off and the duplex was completely naked, I drove over and noticed the rafters at the back of the house needed to be shored up. It needed about $300 worth of wood, which was pretty expensive. By the time it was over, I had to buy nearly forty two-by-fours.

The roofer pulled me aside and said, "It's going to be an extra $500, and you will need to pay for the material."

"No problem." I wanted to use this contractor. He was different from the other roofers. With other roofers, I was usually in control. I'd buy the material and have it delivered. I would double-check the squares. But this contractor handled the whole transaction. I wanted to hire him, let him do his work, and move on.

He got on the project, reinforced the roof, and everything looked great from a distance. I wrote a partial check of $8,700, which included some of the woodworking. I noticed some problems with the fascia and soffit work. He gave me a quote to take care of those, but I would not pay until the work was complete.

But that's not the moral of the story. About two or three weeks later, my ceiling caved in.

Apparently, this "great carpenter" the roofer used on a regular basis didn't put all the weight of the bearing roof on a stem wall. He attached it to any rafter he could find, and the weight pushed down and damaged the entire ceiling. What do you do when your new duplex falls down around you? You call the contractor and matter-of-factly say, "You need to get your behind over here and fix this thing." I had another contractor look at the duplex, and he pointed out all the shoddy work.

I still owed the carpenter $500 for the exterior work. Withholding the $500 may have been the only savvy thing I did. The carpenter came out and was mad we were telling him his work was terrible. He wasn't inclined to correct the work as he had already gotten his paycheck from the roofer. As far as he was concerned his work was done. I don't know if the roofer had big enough balls to slap the dude around, but it needed to be done.

The situation was unbelievably stressful. We argued for forty-five minutes before I told him, "Man, just leave. Get off the property and go." I hired the contractor who pointed out the problem. He strengthened the roof and put it on a stem wall.

Here's the takeaway. Go with your gut and monitor everything. Things will not always go as planned, and you need to be prepared for that. Get every single detail in writing. If you don't, you're going to suffer and pay for it in the long run. (By the way, I didn't pay the guy the remaining $500, which upset the roofer for some reason.)

Nothing good came out of that deal. I learned to always get another opinion. Always talk to someone else. Do your due diligence, and before you're about to say yes, call one more person.

Cover Yourself

I purchased a property and replaced almost everything on the inside. It was a serious rehab. The sewer line on the outside appeared new and recent. Not long after I rented the place the tenant started calling me and saying the sewer line was backing up. I called a plumber, and he came over and snaked it out. Six weeks later, the tenant called back and said, "The sewer is bubbling up outside in the yard."

I called the same plumber to fix it. He told me he had to open the line up to figure out what the problem was, and I gave him the okay. He dug a ditch and fished the line, and said I needed to install a cleanout, which I did. I wasn't happy about spending the cash, but it had to be done. I wrote the check and thought it was taken care of.

A few weeks later, I got another call from the tenant with the same complaint. I sent the same plumber to go look at it. He dug deeper into the line and started pulling out something that was blocking the line. What was the problem? Thirty condoms were stuck in the sewer line.

The plumber called me and said, "I figured out the problem. My work was fine. The tenant is causing the problem." He told me about the condoms.

I was ticked off. I had sent the contractor out there and paid him three times. My next step was to call the tenant and find out what in the world was going on.

I got the tenant on the phone and said, "The contractor dug thirty condoms out of the sewer line and left them in your backyard."

The tenant was a little ticked off. "My wife and I don't use condoms," he blurted out.

"Well, we haven't been putting condoms down the sewer line." The tenant told me he had no intention of paying for the plumber's work.

I was caught in a debate between the plumber and the tenant. I didn't know what to do. Who was I supposed to believe?

It wasn't long before the line backed up again. The plumber dug up the majority of the line, fixed it, and I added those costs to the repairs on the property.

I kept using the same contractor because I wanted to get a discount for being a repeat customer. He did credit my bill and didn't charge me for one visit to the property, but it was too little too late. I was frustrated the cleanout wasn't added to the first visit. That's why I hired him. He was the expert and should have corrected the problem as quickly as possible.

What I learned through this experience is to keep every receipt from each individual contractor. If you use the same contractor over and over again, you can use the receipts to try to get the contractor to warranty his work. If the same problem keeps happening, I wave the receipts in front of him and ask, "Why hasn't this been taken care of yet?"

I scan every invoice I receive and store them in PDF files arranged by contractor. This allows me to go back and see when I hired the contractor, what went wrong, and if I am paying for the same repair over and over again.

When you keep track of what you're spending, you see a pattern evolve. You can say, "On September 15, you went out there and cleaned the line, and now it's December 15 and you're cleaning the same line. What's the deal?" If you approach them that way, contractors tend to work with you to solve the problem, and they might give you a discount or knock something off the bill if they have to go out there again.

One contractor gave me a $75 discount because he had to go back out to do the same work twice in a few months. Arm yourself with receipts and invoices and know specific dates. Print those out so when your contractor comes for the second repair and says, "Your bill's $350 to put in a cleanout," you can respond, "I already paid for this in September." It may make him defensive, but it shows he is being watched. It's a gentle way to remind him, "I hire you for a lot of jobs. You've got to do me right on this one."

MERRY CHRISTMAS

I found a father-son woodworking team on Craigslist. I needed some elaborate woodworking on a banister in a three-story building. It wasn't a task my handyman could do, and it wasn't a job where you could throw up some two-by-fours and make a railing. The job needed skilled individuals to do it right.

After I found their ad, I called them and they met me. The son was a little cocky as he explained that he was working for another contractor making $10 an hour but wanted to venture off on his own. I asked the right questions such as, "Where did you come from? Where are you getting work?" And they were giving me all the information I wanted to know.

We looked at what needed to be done, and the son talked the language.

He knew exactly what he was doing, and he quoted me a rate. He said he would like to make $15 an hour for himself and for his father.

"That's $30 an hour. I need a price for this job."

He looked at his dad and told me, "Five hundred dollars, and you provide the material."

"No problem." He gave me a laundry list of very high-end wood. He wanted specific nails and things I had never purchased before. I could tell in my gut he had the skills and he knew what he was doing. They agreed to start the next day. He said they would be done in a day and a half, but it took three days. They did a phenomenal job. It was perfect, way above my expectations.

"I finally found a contractor I can use, and he can do anything," I thought. The only problem was he wanted to work with his dad, and when I started crunching the numbers $30 an hour for the team was pricey. I didn't want to reveal how big of an empire I had, so I fed him along and asked him to bid another job.

I had the son meet me at a property, and we went through it and looked at everything that needed to be done. It really needed exterior work, and there was a shed in the back that needed to be roofed. It also needed siding, and I asked him if he could do that.

"Yes, we can do that for $700." These guys went to work and did another great job, including replacing all the siding. They removed all the brick, because I wanted to re-side the front, which was separating from the corner. You could see the inside from outside, and it needed a very skilled contractor to shore and button it up and then re-side it.

I worked with him for about a week on this job, and he did outstanding work on the exterior. I was going to have my handyman do the interior, but because these guys were doing such a good job I figured they could handle it.

When he finished the exterior work, he wanted $600. The whole job was $700, and he said, "You can pay me the other hundred when we do the shed."

Normally, I don't pay until the whole job is done, but it was early winter and the weather was getting cold. I gave him $600, which satisfied him and made me feel like I was getting a bargain. It was close to $1,200 worth of work as far as I was concerned. The shed still wasn't done, but I felt confident it would be.

Right before Thanksgiving, it started getting really cold, and he was asking for more work. I was pressed for time, and instead of sending my handyman to install the doors and blinds on the inside, I had the contractor bid on the job. He quoted me a decent fee, and I gave him $400 to purchase some trim and a door. That's when things started falling apart.

I thought this guy was rock solid. He did two impressive jobs for me and we were on the third one. I was under a bit of a crunch because I was trying to get this house rented, which was tough to do during the holidays. I talked to the contractor and he told me they were heading to the property on Monday of Thanksgiving week. I went to the property, but they never showed. All their tools and supplies were there, but I never saw them. He did go to the store and purchase the materials, but that's all he did.

I let it slide until after Thanksgiving and called him during the first week of December. "When are you going to get this job done?"

"We're on it this week."

"Okay." I still hadn't seen him by the 7th of December so I called him again. "Hey, guys, what's going on? I've driven by the property, but I haven't seen you working."

He said his wife was ill and was in the hospital. I told him I understood that things happen and to keep me in the loop.

I thought I'd found a really good contractor. He had done two good jobs, but now things where getting sketchy. Was his wife really sick?

I let a week go by, and I texted him. "When are you guys going to get back out there?" I also expressed concern for his wife.

"We're going to get on it next week." I assumed he was going to be there on Monday. I went out but he never showed up. Then he stopped answering my calls and disappeared.

By now it was Christmas week. I waited three weeks to be nice, as I thought he wanted the work. When I added up all the material he purchased, it was short.

"I need my money back. Call me," I texted him. The contractor refused to call me but he did send a text message stating, "We did work, and that money was for work."

Hiring Contractors

It doesn't matter if it's Christmas or if people are in the hospital. Never give any money to a contractor for work he hasn't done unless you want to lose it. I trusted that guy because he seemed legitimate, he communicated, but something went wrong. I don't even know if he was truthful about his wife, but he could have sent his father to get the work done. I got sucked in, and the job didn't get done. I lost the cash I gave him and had another needless delay. I had to hire another contractor to finish the project, which cost me another month of holding costs and a bunch of drama.

These days I never pay a contractor until all the work is done. If I give him anything before the end of the job, it's very minimal, maybe gas money to get the work finished. I tell him he will have a good payday when it's done. I generally pay on a percentage basis. Some contractors lose motivation near the end of the job. That's the most critical time, because I'm a starter, not a finisher. I need contractors who are finishers because it's the end product that matters.

I think about that story every time I visit that property. The work on the shed was never completed. Tenants have moved in, but they can't use the shed because it leaks. I came out ahead on the deal, but it's frustrating to look at something that should have been done a year ago. Don't let this happen to you.

I Found a Good Guy

I bought a property that had been vacant for so long when I called the city to turn on the water they didn't know the address. It had water at one time, but before I could rent it, the city had to dig a new water main to the property. It was built in 1926 and nothing had been updated. I had to rehab almost everything in it.

I found a young contractor who was a good guy. He'd done some small maintenance work on other properties, but this was a $25,000 project and he wanted to be the lead on it. After I thought about it, I decided to let him do the work. He seemed like a good guy, and I felt like he would be the one who could get the job done.

One of the first things that had to be done was to rewire the entire property. The contractor suggested we use a friend of his who was in his twenties. The contractor told me he was an apprentice for an electrical company and could do all the wiring.

I asked, "How much does your friend charge?"

"He charges $15 an hour."

I ran the numbers and knew we would save thousands of dollars by using his friend. I told the contractor to call his friend and get him to work.

The guy came out and ran brand new wiring throughout the property. Everything was going well, but we still needed to turn on the electricity. The only problem was that we didn't have a permit. The guy figured out how to get the meter base turned on, which gave us electricity throughout the property.

It eventually came time to do an inspection. I called the inspector, and he came out, looked things over, and flagged the property. The inspector told us the wiring wasn't grounded properly and that there were exposed wires. I was screwed.

I called the contractor and went off. "Your friend didn't know what he was doing. We didn't pass inspection. I can't get the electricity turned on without that." The contractor had the electrician come out, and they got into a fight. I could see all the time and money I had invested on the property being flushed own the toilet.

The contractor removed the wires and put in the proper ground, which solved the problems the inspector found. But the city required another inspection, and that meant I would have to pay another inspection fee. It was also going to cost me all the time I spent waiting because I couldn't do anything without the inspection. I couldn't rent the place, so I was paying all my holding fees with no way to generate revenue.

When the inspector called me back, it was one of the weirdest phone calls I have ever received. "I don't know what your guys are doing over here, but they're having way too much fun, and you can't do this," he said and hung up on me.

It finally hit me that the bargain I had paid for was not bargain at all and that I needed to hire a licensed electrician to take care of the problem. I thought about it for a few days and then, out of the blue, I received a phone call from a licensed electrician.

I asked him who he was and he said, "My name is Lawrence. I was talking to your inspector about the problems you're having on your property, and I wanted to see if I could help you in any way."

"How did he get my number?" I thought. "Is it even legal for an inspector to refer an electrician?" I was frustrated, didn't know if I could trust this guy, and I was about to hang up on him. Then I thought, "I've got to get this done."

I had called several other electricians who weren't interested in the work because an unlicensed person had done the work. Contractors don't like the idea of following someone else and cleaning up their mess. I didn't have anything to lose so I asked him to meet me at the property.

He started pointing out all the things that were wrong. The wrong wire was used to feed the box. It was a 200-amp box, and it was running on the wrong gauge wire. The property needed a new weather head. I didn't know what was going to happen, and all I could see was my cash flow drying up.

I asked how much all this was going to cost, and he replied, "I have to run the numbers. I'll get back with you on the price."

I walked back with him to his truck and started asking him the normal questions. "How long you've been doing this? How'd you get into this business? Where did you come from?" Then I had to ask him what I really wanted to know. "How did you get my mobile number?"

This is the funny part. This licensed electrician did a lot of work in the part of the city where my property was located. He had pulled tons of permits, and he had a relationship with the inspector. Because the electrician did so much work in that part of town, the inspector assumed he had done the work on my property. He called the electrician and yelled at him. "You screwed up this job. What's wrong with you?"

The electrician kept his cool and calmly told the inspector, "No, that's not my job." Then he was savvy enough to find out who owned the property. He did some research, found my name, and called me.

That showed me he was motivated, which in turn motivated me. He gave me a bid that was more expensive than I thought it was going to be. I asked him for a discount and then I told him about all the drama I endured and that there would be the chance for more work from other investors.

"Here's the deal. You need all new stuff. Most of the expense is for materials." He broke the bid down in detail. The bid was for $1,500. Five hundred dollars of it was for material and $1,000 was for his time, including pulling the permits. To make a long story short, I used him. The property passed on the first inspection, and I was able to rent it out and start cash flowing on the property.

Here are the takeaways. Sometimes when you cut corners on projects, it's going to take longer and it's going to cost you more money. Some bargains won't be bargains in the long run. I probably broke even on that situation. I may have saved $500 running the wire myself, but ultimately using an unlicensed electrician caused weeks of delays and frustrations.

The young contractor was trying to help me. My goal was trying to save money, but it turned into a disaster.

I usually don't recommend contractors, but this guy has to be known.

His name is Lawrence and he's with Good Guy's Electric. You can find him online or text or call me, and I will give you his number. He has worked on several jobs for me and has always given me a fair price. Through this debacle, I found a great electrician, and I'm going to hold on to him as long as I own properties.

Fun With Foundation

I purchased a property for $5,000 and thought I couldn't go wrong. I did a quick inspection, walked around inside, and it looked like a great deal. Everything seemed fine. There was some minor work to do on the foundation, but it didn't look like a big issue.

I closed on the property a week later and got the keys. To my surprise, there was more work than I could have imagined. I started with the foundation.

The foundation was one of the worst I've ever seen. You could see four- or five-inch gaps under the doors, from the front door to the bedroom doors. I was borderline intimidated by this. One good thing was that it had a subfloor and there was enough room to crawl underneath.

I called my trusted handyman, and he came out. He shook his head and told me, "This is too far gone. This is going to be a monster. Dump this property."

That was not what I wanted to hear. I was running out of options, so I put the property up for sale but didn't get many bites. I was screwed. There was nothing I could do besides fixing the property myself to get it rent-ready or sell it to another investor down the road.

I called a handyman I use for random jobs to get his opinion. He had no experience with foundations but was confident he could get the work done. "It's no big deal. You just jack it up. Throw a twist jack underneath and you're good to go."

I was relieved to hear that the problem could be easily resolved, and I said, "I'll take care of the labor. I'll pay the jacks. How much would you charge me?"

"Three hundred dollars."

"That sounds good. Let me get back with you," I told him.

I wanted another opinion and called a contractor who had installed subflooring, tiled a floor, and installed some kitchen cabinets on another property I owned. He looked at the foundation and told me, "If you pay for all the material, it's going to be $900."

I told him I would get back to him and started thinking about the bids. I had one bid for $300 from a gentleman I trusted but he didn't know what he was doing and another bid for $900 from a guy that I kind of liked but who sometimes rubbed me the wrong way. He could be pushy and aggressive and called me when he needed work. He gave me the impression he was confident and that he had done foundation work before.

"I've got to get this done as soon as possible. The longer that I wait on this job, the more my holding costs will be, and then winter's going to come," I thought. I was afraid that if I didn't do the job soon, I might never get it done. "Go ahead and do it," I told the guy who gave me the $900 bid.

He started working on the project the next day. The interesting thing is he kept sending me photos. He told me to come to the property the following day to look at his work.

When I showed up, he said, "The whole plate on the bottom was destroyed by termites and needs to be replaced. We have to replace a bunch of two-by-fours and it's going to be elaborate."

"No problem, just get it done."

I should have seen something coming. Before Labor Day, he showed up at the office. He said, "I want to get some money."

"Is the job done?"

"No."

"We don't pay until after the job is finished." His request was a red flag. There were several other red flags but I ignored them, which was not a savvy thing to do.

I went home and enjoyed my holiday weekend. Tuesday rolled around and the contractor showed up unannounced at the office with a $1,200 invoice. Prior to him starting the job, I had given him $200 cash for material and provided him the twist jacks.

"Wait a minute. We did not agree to this. Plus, I haven't seen receipts for the cash I gave you." He got really upset with me and said he did more work than he agreed to do, so I whipped out my phone. "Here is a text message where you agreed to do the job for $900. I've never had a contractor agree upon a job and then raise the price by a third. That's outrageous. On top of that, you quoted me for the whole rehab for $10,000. Twelve hundred dollars is more than 10 percent of the whole job, and that includes electrical, plumbing, flooring, and sheet rock. You think you are going to charge me $1,200 for the foundation?"

I was irate and needed to stop talking before I said something I would regret forever. I took a breath, gathered my thoughts, and told him, "I have to go look at the job and take pictures. I'll get back with you." He was frustrated with me because he felt he had done the work that needed to be done. I was mad because he never contacted me to say, "It's going to be $300 more."

The guy continued to pester me. He started blasting me with texts and phone calls. I put the guy on ice. "My hands are tied. I've got to go look at the property. I've got several meetings today," I told him.

I drove to the property and was shocked to see a pile of rubble on the yard and another inside the house. It looked like a decent amount of work had been done, but I was torn about what to do. I wanted to have the whole project done for $600 plus material, and I was in a conflict over a $1,200 invoice. I thought $900 was overpriced, but I was in a hurry to get the job done and had agreed to that amount. I was bummed about the situation.

The guy showed up the next day with a "corrected" invoice, which included a message on the bottom saying he did the work for free. This was one of those situations where I learned a lesson the hard way. I was fed up with the guy and never wanted to see him again, so I paid the $900 and sent him packing.

When everything was done, I thought about why this guy was able to push me around. I was in a hurry and didn't write the job down in detail. As a real estate investor, you have to be the one who takes the initiative, and I dropped the ball. Before you hire anyone, pull out a statement book and write down exactly what he's going to do.

The real problem was that our expectations were different. When he quoted me $900, I thought he was going to do more than just the foundation. I thought he was going to repair the foundation and the subflooring in the bathroom, which still needs work. By the time I paid him, I was $900 over budget and two weeks behind schedule because of the time I spent being jerked around by this unscrupulous contractor.

Learn from my mistakes. Get every agreement in writing, and make sure the contract clearly states what the contractor is being hired to do. Don't leave anything to chance.

THE QUEST

Every time I visit with someone who needs work done on his properties, the conversation always turns to how difficult it is to find someone who will do good work at a decent rate. I've been asked, "How do you find a good contractor?" a thousand times.

Finding a good contractor takes work. You are not going to trip over one of them on your way to the bathroom (unless he happens to be tiling your floor at the time). It can be so challenging I devoted an entire section of *301 Questions with Real Answers for Every Savvy Real Estate Investor* to finding a good contractor.

The best way to find a good contractor is to talk to other investors. If you are active in your local real estate investment club, you will probably be able to pry the name of a reliable contractor from one of the other members. But it may not be easy. Finding a good contractor is like having a winning lottery ticket, and other investors may not be willing to give it up without a fight. If you happen to have the name of a great contractor, be prepared for others to ask you to share.

You can also post ads on Craigslist. I like using technology to build my business. There is no other way you can reach as many people as quickly and cheaply as you can on the Internet.

Here are a few of the most common questions I am asked about hiring contractors. The answers came from my experience, as well as the experience of dozens of other investors I have talked to over the years. Don't try to reinvent the wheel when you hire someone to work for you. Learn from those who have gone before you and take your business to another level.

1. SHOULD I PAY A CONTRACTOR UP FRONT?

This is a tough question. Nine times out of ten, I would say no. It's hard for me to pay anyone before the job is done. I've been burned too many times, and I have heard too many horror stories from other investors. I feel much more comfortable paying for things once I know the work is done and the property is ready for a tenant to move in.

But there are a few situations where I am willing to pay up front. If I have used a contractor before, he has done great work, and he is willing to offer a discount if he is paid up front I might make an exception. The contractor is going to have to explain to me why it's worth it to me to pay him up front.

At times I have paid in stage I may pay 20 percent to start the project, 30 percent when the contractor completes an important part of the project near the halfway point, and the remaining 50 percent when the job is done. That gives me the comfort of knowing the contractor isn't fully paid until the job is done.

2. WHAT'S A SUBCONTRACTOR, AND DO I PAY THEM DIRECTLY?

A subcontractor is someone hired by a general contractor to do a specific job. If you are doing a major rehab, you might hire a general contractor who will hire a plumbing subcontractor, a drywall subcontractor, or an electrical subcontractor.

It is the general contractor's job to pay his subcontractors out of the fee you pay him. That's the benefit of using a general contractor on a big job. He negotiates a single price with you to do all the work, and it's his responsibility to pay for all the labor and materials. It defeats the purpose of hiring a general contractor if you have to deal with subcontractors directly.

3. DO I HAVE TO PULL ANY NECESSARY PERMITS OR DOES THE CONTRACTOR DO THAT?

This is also the contractor's job. If you are going to build an empire, you have to learn to delegate. Don't waste your time pulling permits after you pay a contractor to do the job for you.

But there is a trick some landlords use to save money. Suppose one of their properties needs to be rewired. They will wire the house themselves (or use cheap labor to do it), and then get a meter base permit. That will be enough to get the electricity turned on at the property. Then the landlord will hire a licensed electrician to inspect the wiring and make sure it meets code.

4. How do I get someone to guarantee his work?

Getting a contractor to guarantee his work is really easy. All you have to do is call Bigfoot, take him to the Tooth Fairy's house on your unicorn, and have a few drinks. That will solve everything.

Contractors are not going to guarantee their work. It's never going to happen. They may say they will, but getting them to do it is like pulling teeth. There are some companies that claim to warranty their work, but in my experience, that is nothing but a marketing gimmick. The company I use for foundation work offers a guarantee. I had to call them once, but they never came to the property. I realized that the only thing their written guarantee was good for was to pass on to the next guy when I sold the property.

5. Should I pay for material directly or have the contractor bill me?

This is another tough question. There is no right or wrong answer. I handle these situations differently depending on the facts. I generally prefer for the contractor to buy material and then bill me, but sometimes I will go online and buy the material through a local home supply store's website. The contractor can drive over, load the material into his truck, and deliver it to the job site.

The key issues are: What is your time worth? At what level is your business? Do you only have a few properties, or are you juggling dozens or hundreds of units?

How long I have known the contractor also makes a difference. If I have known him for a long time, I might loan him my credit card and let him take it to the store to purchase supplies. This doesn't happen very often, and when it does, I keep it under tight control. I even go online and make sure the spending limit on the card is only a few dollars more than the supplies will cost. At the end of the day, remember that this is your money and you have a responsibility to control it. You have to be militant or you will get screwed because some people can't handle the temptation of using someone else's credit card.

6. **A CONTRACTOR THREATENED TO PUT A LIEN ON MY HOUSE. WHAT DOES THAT MEAN? CAN I PROTECT MYSELF?**

If you ever hear a contractor say the words "lien" and "your house" in the same sentence, keep your ears open and your mouth shut. Take liens very seriously because they can quickly impair your title and take a bite out of your company.

A lien is a legal instrument that secures your property for a debt the contractor alleges you owe. They are often called mechanics and materialmen's liens. They protect a contractor who alleges you didn't pay for the work he performed or a supplier who alleges a contractor didn't pay for the supplies he used on your property.

You can solve many of these problems by being proactive. When you pay a contractor, use a check or get a receipt that reflects the work was paid for in full. You can also have the contractor sign a lien waiver, which states he has been paid and that he has paid his suppliers.

Don't let anyone take even a small part of your business. You have worked too hard to build it, and you don't want to throw it away because you did business with an unscrupulous contractor.

7. **HOW SHOULD I PAY FOR MATERIALS? SHOULD I USE CASH, A CREDIT CARD, OR STORE CREDIT?**

I prefer to pay with a credit card. It's easy to track and it makes it easier to document your expenses when tax time rolls around.

Sometimes, the contractor will pay cash and I will reimburse him when he drops off the supplies. When this happens, I always check the receipt and make sure it matches the product. You don't want to pay top dollar for the new supplies listed on the receipt when the products in the back of the contractor's truck are three years old. This has been known to happen. Keep your eyes open.

Eventually, you will have a contractor who will tell you, "I have some material left over from another job and can give you a great rate." What he is really telling you is that he stole the material from the last investor he worked for. The investor paid for it, and now the contractor is using it for his own benefit. Be careful about these great deals. If a contractor is willing to steal from another investor, he will steal from you.

Hiring Contractors

8. WHICH IS THE BETTER PLACE TO FIND A CONTRACTOR, CRAIGSLIST OR THE YELLOW PAGES?

Yellow Pages? Did someone invent a time machine while I was asleep and transport me back to 1979?

My preference is Craigslist. It's current, cheap, and it allows you to have instant feedback. I do know people who carry the Yellow Pages around in their trucks, just in case they need them. It's a good plan in case you get passed by a silver DeLorean driven by Michael J. Fox.

9. SHOULD I TAKE BEFORE AND AFTER PHOTOS?

Yes. Be a photo fanatic. Take so many pictures that people think you are a tourist trying to capture as many memories as you can before you board the plane to go home. When it comes to documenting your property and the work you paid a contractor to do, you can't take too many pictures. Digital memory is dirt cheap, and snapping a few dozen pictures won't cost you a quarter. It's better to have the pictures and not need them than to need them and not have them.

10. WHAT IF SOMEONE FALLS OFF A LADDER WHILE WORKING ON MY HOUSE?

Hopefully, he will pick himself up and have a great story to tell his buddies. Anytime you have someone working on your property, you need to think about liability. Actually, you need to start thinking about that the day you buy your first property. An important part of building your empire is making sure you have the right amount of insurance when you own your first house. If you don't visit with your insurance agent and get the right coverage when you start investing, you will regret it. Don't let anyone on your property with a ladder, chainsaw, or power equipment without discussing liability with your insurance agent.

Be sure any contractors you hire sign a worker's compensation release before they start working. Don't let them step one inch on your property without having a waiver that clearly states they are independent contractors and have a worker's compensation insurance policy in their name.

Another great idea is to carry an incident report form. This should include a space for the date, time, and address of the property, as well as a section where you can fill out a detailed report of what the worker claims happened. Take thorough notes, and include a description of the area and how the worker was acting. If he claims he broke his leg, ask another worker, "Did he stand on his own and walk to the company truck without any help?" Once you fill out the report, have the worker who claims to be injured sign it. Take pictures of the property (especially the area where the worker claims to have been hurt) and the worker.

You will be amazed at how many people will try to take the easy way out and see a worker's comp injury as an easy payday. Protect yourself and your business by documenting everything.

11. WHAT IF THE WORK FALLS APART SIX MONTHS AFTER THE CONTRACTOR IS FINISHED?

Write this in stone. It's going to happen. As soon as the check clears the bank, one of the projects you paid for will fall apart. You will watch your hard-earned money go up in smoke and there won't be anything you can do.

This is one of the reasons it is so important to make sure you hire the right contractor at the start of your project. You get what you pay for most of the time, and if you don't do your homework and choose the wrong contractor, you will end up paying for the same work twice.

To put it bluntly, there won't be much you can do when work falls apart before it should. If the contractor is willing to honor his word, you might be able to get him back to the jobsite and look at the work. But even then, you are likely to hear him say it is normal wear and tear and he won't be willing to do anything.

I did have one contractor agree to come back and repair shoddy work he had done, but he was offered another job and never got back to me. In all the contracting jobs I've had done over the years, that is as close as I have been to having someone stand behind his work.

Avoid this problem by hiring the right person for the job and making sure it is done properly before you pay in full.

12. WHAT IF I WANT TO SUE A CONTRACTOR?

I have had a lot of time to think about this because I have sat in many courtrooms waiting to sue people. What I am about to tell you is the wisdom I gained by watching countless people stand in front of judges.

Going to court is a waste of time and money, and it sucks your energy and cash. No one makes money at the courthouse. If you are at the courthouse, you are taking time away from building your empire. Which would you rather do: watch the clock click slowly by as you wait for your case to be called, or close a multi-million dollar deal on new properties? You can always hire an attorney to do the dirty work for you, but that gets expensive.

Of course, we have to have courts to settle disputes. The alternatives (such as having a duel in the town square at dawn or chopping the hand off a thief) aren't any better. But even if you get a judge to rule in your favor, the case isn't over. You will have to find a way to make the other person pay (if damages are awarded) or leave the property (if you are granted an eviction).

Your focus should never be on how to win in court. Your focus should be on how to avoid a battle. If you have to file a lawsuit, you have already lost. When hiring a contractor, this means making sure you do due diligence and hire the right person for the job.

13. What paperwork and ID should a contractor provide before he starts work?

As much he is willing to give. Make sure you can document who worked for

Hiring Contractors

you, what your agreement was, and who is going to pay if things fall apart. Start with his insurance, license, and proof of worker's comp coverage. Be sure to take his picture. If he agrees to it, I would take a DNA swab, yank out a follicle of his hair, have him fingerprinted, ask for a credit report, and hold his parents as collateral. They can go home six months after the work is completed, assuming it doesn't fall apart before that.

14. WHAT IF THE WORK DOESN'T PASS INSPECTION?

Some work will have to be inspected by local authorities, such as plumbing, electrical, and heating and ventilation. If the work doesn't pass, you may not be able to rent the property and you may have a hard time selling it. It's important to know what needs to be inspected and what doesn't. If you have any questions about this, ask your mentor or someone in your local real estate investors' association.

The best way to avoid this problem is to make the final payment on the project contingent upon the work passing inspection. The contractor doesn't get paid until the inspector signs off on the work. That is the best carrot to make sure the work is done and up to code. If you pay before the inspector approves it, you won't have any leverage to make the contractor show up and get the work done properly.

15. WHO ARRANGES INSPECTIONS?

Work is done in three stages. The first step is where the contractor pulls any necessary permits to get the job done. The next step is the actual project, where the electricity is rewired or the plumbing is repaired. The final step is the inspection process.

The contractor normally arranges any inspections. Keep in mind that one of the best reasons to hire a contractor is to leverage your time. Which call is going to make you more money: one to the city inspector or one to a prospective tenant? Don't step over dollars to get to dimes. Spend your time on the things that are going to bring the greatest return. Plus, you hired the contractor to take care of details like inspections. Let him earn his money.

A good contractor will know more about regulations and code than you will. If a contractor handles the inspection, he can answer any questions the inspector has and can demonstrate why the work is up to code. And if the work doesn't pass, he can change it immediately or arrange for it to be done as soon as possible.

16. Do I have to hire a licensed plumber to change a faucet in my kitchen?

It sounds crazy to me, but some places require a licensed plumber to do simple jobs, such as changing a faucet. It's easy and homeowners do it every day. But the law in your area may require a licensed plumber to do even the most basic work on rental property.

Generally, whether or not a license is required depends on the permits issued and the scope of the job. I use a handyman for as many projects as I can because prices skyrocket as soon as someone with a license gets involved. The savvy thing to do is to avoid paying for licensed contractors unless absolutely necessary.

17. Should I pay for an estimate?

Never, ever pay for an estimate. If any contractor tells you he charges for estimates, hang up the phone and call the next one on your list. No reputable contractor charges for estimates, and if one asks you for money for the privilege of coming out to inspect your property he is either a thief or takes you for a fool. Don't do business with people like that.

18. Can a handyman build my new add-on bedroom?

You will be tempted to try this. You will have a handyman who is great at his job. He shows up on time, does what he says he is going to do, and gets things done. If he finds out you need to build on to one of your properties he will offer you a ridiculously low price to do it.

You need to be aware of these offers. A handyman is not skilled, experienced, or licensed to undertake a large project like an addition. They know how to play the game and will try to talk you into letting them do major projects for you. Don't fall for it. Hire only licensed, experienced contractors to do large projects. You will thank me later.

19. What if the project is half done and suddenly the price goes up?

You are screwed and at the contractor's mercy. He is on your property, the walls or floors are torn up, there is no way you can fire him, and he knows it. Prepare yourself because if you are in the real estate investment game long enough, this will happen to you. It's not a question of "if." It's a question of "when."

This is one of the reasons you have to have a written agreement on every project. A handshake deal won't protect you when a contractor decides that he hasn't charged you enough.

Whenever a contractor tells you the price to finish a job will be higher than the one he quoted, you need to make him justify the increase before you pay an additional penny. There might be circumstances that justify an increase, such as unexpected damage that could not be seen until he started working. If that happens, make sure you inspect the area to see if any additional cost is justified. Take pictures if you need to and e-mail or text them to an experienced friend you trust who can offer insight.

Make sure you express your displeasure and how uncomfortable you feel about the increase. If you don't, you will be writing checks every day.

20. How many estimates should I get before hiring a contractor?

You should get at least three bids on every project, but the more the better. Three or four bids should give you an idea of the price range of your project.

When you are looking at bids, always remember the difference between price and value. The cheapest bid is not always the best. You may save money on the front end by going with the low bid, but if the bid is too low for the contractor to reasonably do a good job, you will end up paying more in the long run.

21. How does the bid process work?

What happened to the tough questions? You were doing great. Don't start lobbing softballs now.

The bid process is straightforward. Contractors come to your property, look at what needs to be done, and give you an estimate.

Make sure that the contractor actually inspects the property. He won't know how much work needs to be done if he doesn't look at it in person. Anyone who gives you an estimate over the phone or by e-mail won't understand the scope of the project and his bid may be too low (which may frustrate him in the long run because he can't do the work he promised for the price he quoted) or too high (which will tick you off). If he's not willing to drive to your property and inspect it, hire someone else.

It's also important that you get every bid in writing. You will need that in case there is a dispute. Any decent contractor won't have a problem giving you a written bid. If he refuses, it's a giant red flag and you proceed with him at your peril.

22. What if the contractor demands to be paid in cash and refuses a check?

Be afraid. Be very afraid. When someone only wants to do business in cash, an alarm should go off in your head and you should see giant flashing stop signs. This is a sign of bigger issues. Is he trying to hide the cash from the taxman? Has a supplier sued him and gotten a judgment against him? Does he have a substance abuse problem and need to pay his dealer?

It is very tempting when a contractor offers you a discount for paying in cash. It means that you are saving money, which improves your cash flow, and that is the name of the real estate investing game.

But paper trails always work the best. Document every deal you make, including when you paid for work. If there is ever a dispute, you won't have a leg to stand on if you did everything under the table on a cash basis.

I carry a receipt book in my truck. If I need to pay someone, I give him a receipt, keep the carbon copy for my records, and sleep well at night knowing I have that documentation. And I always make sure the contractor signs the receipt.

23. Should I let a contractor use recycled parts or materials?

This depends on the job. I am always looking to save money. Reducing my expenses by a few percent each year by using recycled parts and materials translates into thousands of dollars, and that makes me happy. I get warm and fuzzy just thinking about it.

But I have to balance the need to save money with the need to make sure the work will last. Why cut corners on something that could be faulty?

Will I save money in the long run if I use a recycled part that will have to be replaced sooner than a new one?

Whether or not I let a contractor use recycled parts depends on the facts. If I can see the part and know it will work as it should, I may let him install it. At the end of the day, it has to fit within my plan to create positive cash flow.

24. SHOULD THE BID BE AN ESTIMATE OR AN EXACT PRICE?

You could rephrase this question as, "Should I give my contractor a blank check and the PIN number to my ATM card?"

Every bid you receive should be as close to an exact price as possible. If not, you can bet that the "estimates" you receive will escalate. By the time all is said and done, the price you pay won't look anything like the one you were quoted.

On many projects, there are items that may go over the anticipated cost, such as materials. Having an exact price on the bids you receive will help keep those in check and will prevent you from having sticker shock and buyer's regret at the end of the project. It will also make sure that your cash flow stays positive.

25. WHAT DOES "BONDED AND INSURED" MEAN? SHOULD I ONLY HIRE CONTRACTORS WHO ARE BONDED AND INSURED?

"Bonded and insured" is a fancy way of saying that the contractor has insurance that will pay in the event something bad happens on a job, such as if an employee is injured or if he accidently backs his truck into the side of your house.

It's a great slogan to have on the side of a truck, but you have to make sure you get copies of the policies that prove the contractor is covered. Don't let anyone work on your property if he cannot prove he is insured, regardless of what his business card or slogan says.

26. **A CONTRACTOR I'VE NEVER USED IS COMING OVER TOMORROW TO WORK ON MY BATHROOM. SHOULD I HIDE MY VALUABLES?**

Why worry? In fact, why don't you just take everything in your house worth more than $20 and put it in a big pile on your bed. Let the complete stranger get a good look at everything you own. What problem would that cause?

Not all contractors are thieves, but they are all people. People give into temptation, and some people get sticky fingers when they see something shiny and valuable. It looks like candy to them, and they have to put their hand in the jar and take a piece home.

Remove the temptation by making sure that your valuables are out of sight. That way, you won't have to trawl pawnshops looking for the ring your wife's grandmother left her.

27. **WHAT'S SHOULD I DO IF SOME OF MY PERSONAL PROPERTY GOES MISSING AFTER A CONTRACTOR WORKS ON MY PROPERTY?**

You know the routine. You call the police, file a report, and hope that something is found and returned. The contractor will deny anything is missing and accuse you of making the entire thing up. If he took anything with a serial number, you may have a chance of seeing it again, but if he took cash or jewelry (which can be melted down), you are probably out of luck.

Be proactive. Make sure your valuables are out of sight or in a safe place before the contractor comes over. Don't wait for the horse to be stolen before you lock the barn.

Be sure to keep the model and serial numbers from the products you order. If they are stolen, you will need that information to file a police report, and it will make it easier for you to find parts or to get them serviced if necessary.

28. WHAT'S THE DIFFERENCE BETWEEN A COMMERCIAL CONTRACTOR AND A RESIDENTIAL CONTRACTOR?

Specialization. Contractors can work on any project, but some want to specialize on one or the other. The economics of the projects are completely different. It's okay if your contractor does both, as long as he has experience in the area you want. I wouldn't be excited about hiring someone for a residential project if he had tons of commercial experience but no residential. Let the other guy be the guinea pig.

29. WHAT IF THE PROJECT TAKES TWICE AS LONG AS PROMISED?

Let me sit down for a moment. I get a migraine just thinking about this.

This has happened to me and it will happen to you, and it's exasperating. If you don't believe me, ask the guy sitting next to you at your local REIA meeting.

This is another reason you should have a written agreement for every project. Before you begin a project, you and your contractor have to agree on how long the project will take. You need to be on the same page or you will both be disappointed. Your agreement should include a timeline that spells out consequences for delays. If you are paying 50 percent of the fee when the work is done, your agreement should include a clause that reduces the amount for each day or week the project is delayed. Of course, always have these clauses reviewed by your attorney to make sure they are enforceable. You don't want to get to court and have the judge rule that you owe the contractor money even if he didn't finish on time.

30. WHAT IS A REASONABLE MARKUP ON MATERIAL?

Some contractors charge 20 percent. That's a little expensive for me. I don't mind paying 10 percent if the contractor buys material and delivers it to the job site. Regardless of what you pay, get receipts and make sure the product delivered is the one listed.

31. SHOULD I PAY BY THE HOUR OR FOR THE PROJECT?

I always pay per job. I like the certainty of a fixed price. I don't want to get halfway through a project and realize the costs are going to be double or triple what I planned. Paying by the job helps me budget my costs and keeps my cash flowing.

Be prepared that a fixed price may change when the contractor starts the job and starts poking under the foundation or behind the drywall. But don't be a doormat. If the price increases substantially, ask questions and expect honest answers. Don't approve any additional costs until you understand them and why they are needed.

32. SHOULD I HIRE ONE GENERAL CONTRACTOR OR SEVERAL SPECIALTY CONTRACTORS?

Your answer to this question will probably change as you gain experience. The purpose of hiring a general contractor is to hire one person to get large projects done. The general contractor hires the subcontractors, which means you avoid the headache of dealing with them.

It's a great way to do things when you are new and don't have confidence in your ability to maintain, repair, and rehab a property. I'm at the point where I act as my own general contractor. I have years of experience and have worked on hundreds of properties, so I feel comfortable hiring subcontractors and making sure their work is done properly. Hopefully, one day you will feel comfortable enough to be the general contractor on your projects.

Being your own general contractor is more work. In many ways, it would be smarter for me to delegate those responsibilities. I only have so much time in the day, and following up on subcontractors eats into that.

Hiring a general contractor also takes a great deal of trust. He would hold the keys to my business, my money, and my family's future. I haven't found that person yet.

33. WHAT IS ANGIE'S LIST?

Angie's List is a website that helps people find local handymen and contractors. I haven't used it, but the idea is that people can post online ratings of the companies they have used. It's a modern way of giving word-of-mouth advertising. It's another way you can find information about the people you are considering hiring, and I'm all for that.

34. CAN I TRUST THE BETTER BUSINESS BUREAU AND HOW DOES IT WORK?

This is nothing against the BBB, but I don't use it. I think it's an outdated business model. In my opinion, you are better off using social media or websites like Craigslist.

My understanding of the BBB is that contractors can call in, pay to join, and use the BBB logo on their website and marketing material, even if they have never done any work. The BBB has its place, but I think there are better options.

Regardless of what you use, you still need to do your due diligence. Due diligence always pays off, and you can never take it for granted.

35. SHOULD I HIRE MY BROTHER-IN-LAW TO WORK ON MY PROPERTY?

Only if you have a divorce attorney, psychiatrist, and emergency room doctor on speed dial. It is never a good idea to hire family. It rarely ends well, and dealing with a relative changes how you can run your business. Imagine if you have to make the decision to reprimand or fire your brother-in-law. How is that going to play out at the next family reunion?

Hiring and firing is an emotional process even when you are dealing with people you are not related to. Adding the additional dynamic of family ratchets up the pressure and can make things miserable. You have to keep your employees and contractors at arm's length, and it is nearly impossible to do that with family.

I would only consider hiring a family member if he was a licensed, a full-time contractor, and had a long track record of doing high-quality work. I would never hire one to be my flunky. Ordering a family member around to do manual labor is trouble waiting to happen.

36. WHAT IF I DECIDE I DON'T LIKE THE CONTRACTOR AFTER THE WORK BEGINS?

This is another reason you have to perform due diligence before you hire someone. If you take the time to meet with prospective contractors, you can weed out someone that might not be a good fit for you. Spend a little time getting to know the contractors who bid on your projects. It doesn't have to be a lot of time. You can learn a lot about someone even if you only chat with him for a few minutes.

I would have to really dislike someone to fire him in the middle of the project. It's very expensive. You will need to pay the contractor for the work he has performed. Plus, you are going to have to hire someone to finish the job, and that may push the cost of the work higher than what the first contractor would have charged.

I have a high tolerance, and I would rather bite my tongue and let the first contractor complete his work then send the jerk packing. That's a lot easier than firing someone in the middle of the project and finding a replacement.

I also try to find people I can work well with by getting as many people as possible to bid on jobs. When I use Craigslist to post a job, I try to get ten laborers to show up. Of those ten, I keep the two I like the best.

37. SHOULD I GIVE A CONTRACTOR A KEY TO MY PROPERTY?

My general rule is that no one needs a key to one of my properties except for me, my staff, and my tenants. Contractors generally don't need keys.

The one exception I will make is if the property is empty. If so, I will give the contractor a key because it makes it convenient for him. But once his work is done, I change the locks before renting the property again. A lockbox works well, too. This allows the contractor to enter the property when he wants to, and you don't have to be there to hand him the keys. Consider using Landlord Locks.

Hiring Contractors

38. SHOULD I NEGOTIATE UP FRONT AND ASK FOR A DISCOUNT?

Yes. Everything is negotiable, and I try to save money on every project. The worst that can happen is that the contractor tells you no. Be careful about negotiating too aggressively. If you beat the contractor down and he resents how he was treated, he may not give you his best effort. Be tough when you negotiate, but don't push too far or you may lose an ally and someone who could have done great work for you.

39. WHICH PROJECTS SHOULD I HIRE A CONTRACTOR TO COMPLETE, AND WHICH SHOULD I DO MYSELF?

Eventually, you should hire someone to do all the work on your properties. To grow a real estate empire, you have to leverage your time. You may have started your business by doing all the maintenance and repairs, but to take it to the next level you have to stop repairing properties yourself. Hire a contractor who does it every day. The work will be better, and it will be a better investment of your time.

If you don't start subcontracting work, ten years from now, you will still be in the same place you are today. You can't move forward if you try to do everything yourself. You have to think like a mogul to build an empire. Do you think Donald Trump changes the locks or paints the walls at his properties? He doesn't, and neither should you.

40. SHOULD I LET THE CONTRACTOR LEAVE TOOLS AND EQUIPMENT ON THE PROPERTY?

No. I don't want to be responsible if something is stolen or if someone is hurt. It only takes thirty minutes for a contractor to load and unload his tools each day, and you can factor that in if you are paying by hour. Make sure your written agreement states you are not responsible for the contractor's tools.

41. SHOULD I ALWAYS USE THE CONTRACTOR WHO SUBMITS THE CHEAPEST BID?

Not necessarily, but the best bid may be the cheapest. You want the best value. Sometimes that means the cheapest, sometimes that means the most expensive, and sometimes it is one of the other bids.

Best value can be hard to define, but it could be loosely described as the deal that costs the least over the long term. A deal may be inexpensive on the front end, but it's not a good value if you have to repair or re-do the work a few years later. Always look for the best value and not just the lowest cost.

42. WHAT'S THE BEST WAY TO SELECT THE RIGHT CONTRACTOR FOR MY PROJECT?

Have you been reading this book? There are a lot of factors to consider, but it comes down to doing your homework. I spend a lot of time performing due diligence. It is the most important part of the process. I get to know as much as I can about the people I hire. We're going to be working closely together and I want to hire the best contractor I can and make sure he is going to fit in with the rest of my team. Regardless of how great he is at his job or how low his price is, if I don't trust him or we can't work together, I won't hire him.

When it's time to make the call, I go with my gut. Trust your instincts. They will rarely let you down. If you don't feel good at the start of a project, you will feel even worse a month into it. If you have any doubts about a contractor, don't hire him. It's a lot easier to make sure you hire the right contractor before the project begins than it is to hire someone to clean up the mess he left behind.

43. Does the bank or my insurance company need to know what contractor I am using?

This is a touchy subject, and it depends on the project. If you do a major project (like replacing a roof), most banks and insurers will want you to submit the bids so they can document the work you have done on the property. Some banks may even require you to submit receipts.

If you have any doubt, give your bank and insurance company more information than they ask for. It's important to keep them in the loop, and it may help you the next time you go in and ask for money. You don't want your next loan application to be denied because your bank feels you were hiding something.

If you have to file an insurance claim, you will have to give the information to the bank. They will want to make sure you are taking care of the property they hold a lien on.

44. My HOA requires me to hire a contractor to build a fence. Do I have to do that or can I build it myself?

Homeowners' associations have a legitimate reason for doing this. They want to prevent people from doing lousy work that diminishes the value of all the properties in the neighborhood. Any knucklehead can dig a few holes in the ground, stick some posts in them, and attach a few panels of fencing. But that doesn't mean the fence will be done properly.

If you can build a decent fence, you might be able to talk to the HOA and try to get a waiver or exemption. If they deny it, you have to decide if fighting it is worth your time and money. You might be better off hiring someone to do it and moving on to the next project.

45. Do discrimination laws apply to hiring contractors?

You should always consult your attorney about what laws do or don't apply to you. Federal law may allow you to be penalized if you discriminate against a contractor, and there may be other state or local laws as well.

Here are a few thoughts. America is one of the most diverse cultures in the history of the world. As you build your empire, you will encounter people of all races, religions, and backgrounds. You don't have time to discriminate against people, and it will cost you in the long run. It's wrong on every level.

The only color that matters is green. Other than that, be colorblind. Always hire the best value, and you can't go wrong.

46. How long should I wait for a contractor to return my call?

One of the biggest complaints people have about contractors (or anyone in a service industry) is that they don't return phone calls in a timely manner. It's frustrating to leave a message for someone and then wait by the phone for a return call.

I never wait longer than two days for a contractor to return my call. If he doesn't return it by then, I call someone else. Don't waste your time waiting on someone to call when there are dozens of other qualified and hungry people eager to work for you. Time is your most valuable asset, and if you spend it waiting to hear back from people, your empire will never grow.

47. Should I be understanding when my contractor gets called to other projects and the job on my property is put on hold?

Any good contractor will have more than one project going on at a time, and he may have to go from job site to job site to make sure everything is getting done. It's part of the deal. But he has to keep it within reason.

Delays cost investors money. Every day your project is delayed is a day you can't charge rent. You have to put your foot down when other projects are more important to the contractor than yours. Don't settle for being the lowest rung on the ladder. Make sure your contractor knows you are going to hold his feet to the fire if necessary.

48. WHAT PROTECTION DO I HAVE WHEN DEALING WITH A CONTRACTOR?

You have the most protection before you give him any money, and that's why doing your due diligence is important. Once you hand over the check, the balance of power shifts. Arm yourself with the tools in this book, and learn as much as you can before you hire anyone.

49. THE WELL-DRESSED ROOFER I HIRED DOESN'T SHOW UP WITH THE CREW. IS THAT NORMAL?

Yes. This happens all the time, and I would be shocked if it didn't happen that way. The man who brought you the contract is a salesman, and he won't be doing any of the work. You may never see the salesman again, but if you have questions or concerns about the project, you can contact him and get him out to the property.

50. WHAT IS A CHANGE ORDER?

A change order happens when an investor decides to change something about the project once work has commenced. For example, you are rewiring a house and decide to add more outlets in a room or a 220-volt outlet in the garage. You will need to make the change in writing, and you should be prepared to pay extra when you make a change order. Any smart contractor will recognize the extra work and will make sure you are prepared to pay for it.

Hiring Contractors

51. IS IT SAVVY TO HAVE TWO DIFFERENT GENERAL CONTRACTORS ON THE SAME JOB SITE?

This may sound like a good idea. You hire two contractors and think the work will be done more quickly. I can pretty much guarantee two general contractors will fight. They will both want to be in charge, and small things (such as who parks where or who gets to work in a certain area of the project first) will become major issues. If you hire two general contractors to work at the same time, you might find yourself in the middle of a turf war. If the two contractors are working on different trades (if one is working on electricity and one is doing HVAC), it might work. But there may be times when you will need to set boundaries. Remember, the point of hiring contractors and general contractors is to make your life easier. Don't set yourself up for failure by creating a no-win situation.

52. HOW DO YOU KNOW THE GUY GIVING YOU AN ESTIMATE WILL DO A GREAT JOB?

Due diligence always pays off. The only way to make sure that a contractor submitting a bid will follow up on his work and deliver a quality product is to know as much about him as possible before you sign a contract. Ask him as many questions as you can, ask to speak to customers he has worked for in the past, and always trust your gut. My instincts have never let me down, but I have been burned when I didn't listen to my inner voice.

Once you sign a contract and hand over a check, it's going to be too late to do anything, so make sure you hire the right guy the first time. It's the savvy way to do things, and it will help you build your empire as quickly as you can.

53. What happens if the contractor doesn't lock up and your property gets damaged or vandalized?

This is one of those questions where I feel I am painting a negative picture of becoming an investor. I think people might read this and say, "Steven makes investing sound like a lousy way to make a living. I'm not sure I want to put myself and my family through that." Let me throw a little sunshine on this.

Being an investor is one of the greatest things I have ever done. It has given me more freedom and financial opportunity than I could have imagined, and that's why I am sharing my story and the lessons I have learned. I want other people to know the joy of building their companies from the ground up and to be able to spend time with their families. But there are pitfalls, and I want to help you avoid them. Reading about the challenges is the best way to grow your company the right way. That being said, let's get back to answering this question.

If you rehab enough houses, this will happen to you. A contractor will forget to lock a door or a fence and someone will break in and steal or damage property. It's not fun, but it will eventually happen.

The first question you need to ask is whose property was damaged or stolen. Was it the contractor's or yours? If it was the contractor's, it's a no-brainer. He's out of luck. He is responsible for his tools, and if he didn't make sure they were secured before he left for the night, it's not your problem. Any contractor worth his salt will load up his tools in his truck and take them with him every night, and if he doesn't, he will learn a lesson the hard way.

If your property was damaged, the contractor may be on the hook if he forgot to lock up. It's not a bad idea to swing by your property each night when it's being worked on to make sure that the contractor hasn't left the front door wide open. It takes a little time and energy, but not nearly as much as it would to argue about whose fault it is that the property is damaged or that something was stolen.

54. Should I get an itemized bid or one that has a lump sum?

Always make sure to get an itemized bid. It will break down the project in terms of material and labor, and this will allow you to negotiate on each point. When you see what the contractor is charging you for material, you can call around and see if you can get the same items for a lower price. Review what he is charging for labor and see where you can save money. Is he charging you $25 an hour to clean up debris? You can hire guys to do that for $8 an hour. Remember, it's all about cash flow. The more you save on each job, the more you put in your pocket.

55. SHOULD I USE A CONTRACTOR WHO LIVES FIFTY MILES AWAY FROM MY PROPERTY?

You should use the contractor who will give you the best value. There is nothing wrong with hiring a contractor who lives in a different part of town or city than your property. But he needs to be familiar with the area your property is in, and it would be best if he worked there before. He needs to know where the local supply houses are. You don't want him driving two hours to get parts or material he could have purchased three blocks away.

Be sure he is familiar with local building codes and regulations. Things vary from city to city, and you don't his work rejected by a local inspector when you are ready for paying tenants to move in. If he has done great work in the area before and gives a reasonable bid, there shouldn't be any problem hiring him.

56. WHO WILL BE THE ON-SITE FOREMAN? HOW WILL THE PROJECT BE SUPERVISED?

If you hire a general contractor, he's the man. He will be in charge of everything, and you shouldn't have to deal with any of the subcontractors. That's why you are paying him. Make him earn his money.

If you are dealing with subcontractors, you will be responsible for supervising them and making sure the work gets done on time and to your standards. You will save some money because you are not hiring a general contractor, but the flip side is that you have to invest more of your time to get the job done. You also need the confidence to supervise

Hiring Contractors

contractors, and this includes knowing enough about the type of work being performed. Can you look at roof decking or insulation and see if the contractor has made any basic mistakes installing it? If not, you need to make sure you hire the right contractor or a general contractor to handle things for you. Be sure to watch the work being done and ask as many questions as possible. Educate yourself so that the next time you have work done, you can supervise the contractors.

57. SHOULD I ADD A TIMELINE AND A PENALTY?

The only reason you would never include a deadline in your contract (and a penalty if the contractor goes over) is if you want the project to last forever. If you don't have a deadline and consequences for missing it, it won't take long for your contractor to get a call about another project at a different property. He will hop on that and you will never see him again.

Make sure your contractor understands it is in his best interest to finish your project on time. If not, you may end up with plumbing that goes nowhere or wires that don't connect to the power line.

58. WHO TAKES CARE OF THE DEBRIS FROM THE JOB?

The contractor should normally include the cost of any cleanup in his bid. Make sure your contract specifies that he will do so, and make sure it is being done at a reasonable rate. If he is installing a new roof, don't let him charge you the high rates a skilled roofer would command to haul trash from a job site. You may want to hire unskilled workers to do the cleanup, and the contractor can deduct that fee from his bid. Always be looking for ways to be savvy with your money. Pennies turn into dollars, and dollars make the real estate investing world go round.

59. WHAT DO I DO IF A HOUSING INSPECTOR STOPS BY UNANNOUNCED?

Smile, shake his hand, and offer him a cup of coffee or a glass of water. Never be rude, defensive, or angry. Inspectors can make your life miserable if they want to, so you don't want to give them any reason.

I once asked an attorney about practicing law. He said the most important thing about being a successful attorney was being nice to the court clerks and the judges' secretaries. If you are rude to them or treat them like dirt, they have the power to make things unpleasant for you. You wouldn't get to speak to the judge when you need to, and if you needed to schedule a hearing, it might take forever.

You want the inspectors on your side, and you never want to make enemies out of them. Don't give them any reason to delay or deny your inspection. If you own a lot of properties, you may see the same inspector more than once, and you better believe he will remember the time you told him to get off your property. Plus, being decent to people is the right thing to do. It makes a difference in the long run.

60. WHAT IF MY CONTRACTOR DISAPPEARS?

What? A contractor makes a lot of promises, takes your money, and then skips town? I can't believe that would happen. Of course, in my world the sun is always shining, birds are always singing, and I trip over rainbows on the way to the park.

Every year in Oklahoma, we have spring storms. Sometimes, these are really violent and they include severe tornados and hailstorms, which damage a lot of roofs. A soon as the rain stops falling, contractors start crawling out of the woodwork to "help" homeowners who have been hit by Mother Nature. A few months later, there are a slew of stories in the local media about unscrupulous contractors who didn't complete the work people hired them to do. They took the money and left town. It's sad, and it happens over and over again.

The best way to resolve this is to be proactive. If the contractor is gone, it may be too late. Hire the right people by using the tips and techniques I explained earlier, and you will avoid 99 percent of the problems bad contractors create.

If your contractor skips town without finishing your project, contact your attorney and give him all the information you have on the contractor, including the photocopy of his ID you kept for your records. You should also contact your state attorney general and file a complaint as quickly as possible. The truth is that it may be difficult for you to see any of your money again, but at least you can help the next investor.

PUT ME IN, COACH

One of the best things you can do to build your empire is to create a depth chart of contractors you can depend on. You're always one phone call away from any contractor disappearing or never working for you again. The guy might have overcharged you on a repair (and you're done with him), he could be in jail, or his phone might be turned off. The reasons are endless.

Giving all your electrical work to one contractor sounds reasonable and makes you seem like a loyal customer. Many people assume if they're loyal to one electrician he will reciprocate by giving better service and a price break. But this isn't always the case.

One of these days, you will get a call from a tenant telling you her air conditioner is broken. You can hear her child screaming in the background.

You immediately call the HVAC contractor who has done all of your work for the past three years. He's installing new HVAC systems in a 100-room hotel and can't get to your project for three or four days. This is where a depth chart comes into play.

If you're a sports fan, you're familiar with depth charts. Every team has

Hiring Contractors

starters and backup players. If someone gets injured, another player comes off the bench and jumps in the game. Create a depth chart of contractors by making a list of potential hires three people deep. If you can't get in touch with one contractor (or don't want to), move down the list and bring the next player in the game.

RED FLAGS & SCAMS

"I am not bound to win, but I am bound to be true. I am not bound to succeed, but I am bound to live by the light that I have. I must stand with anybody that stands right, and stand with him while he is right, and part with him when he goes wrong."

-Abraham Lincoln

If there were a way to invest in real estate without having to hire contractors, I would do it in a moment. It wouldn't bother me at all to never hire anyone to work on my properties. But that will never happen. Contractors are part of the process. Whenever you hire people to work for you, you will come across some bad apples. Some people will try to cheat and steal from you, and you have to learn how to avoid them.

This section will help you recognize construction scams. Unscrupulous contractors will do whatever they can to make money, and you need to be able to spot when someone is trying to put his hand in your pocket and take what he hasn't earned.

RED FLAGS

Red Flag 1: Discounted Price Because There Are Materials Left Over From His Last Job. If a contractor approaches you and offers to

Hiring Contractors

discount his price because he has materials left over from a previous job you should run (don't walk) the other way. He has stolen material from another investor, and if he does that to another investor, he will do it to you.

Red Flag 2: Offering a Percentage Off the Job Without Being Specific. In some cases, a contractor will not be able to provide you an exact estimate. If you want to remodel your bathroom and need to have the old tiles removed, the contractor is not going to know if the wall behind the tiles will need to be repaired or replaced until the tiles are no longer on the wall.

If they take the tiles off and realize the wall is rotten, they should explain the issue to you and let you make the final decision. No honest contractor is ever going to offer you a percentage off of a completed job without providing details. He could increase the invoice to whatever price he chooses, so that the discount he is offering appears reasonable.

Red Flag 3: The Contractor Does Not Have a Business Card with a Local Phone Number, Address, and State License Number. If a contractor's business card does not have the most basic information on it, find somebody else. You have no idea who you are dealing with.

Red Flag 4: The Contractor Wants to be Paid in Full Before the Job Starts. Most reputable contractors will ask you for a deposit before they start working. Unless it is a very small job, no trustworthy contractor will demand to be paid in full before the job is completed. If a contractor can't afford basic material costs, you shouldn't do business with him.

Red Flag 5: The Contractor Only Accepts Cash. Some good contractors want to be paid in cash, and we all know why. But if they only accept cash and won't let you pay by credit card or check alarm bells should go off. You need to document everything, and if your contractor won't let you do that it's time to find somebody else.

Red Flag 6: The Contractor Will Not Provide a Written Estimate. All honest, reliable contractors provide written estimates. If the one you are negotiating with doesn't, look for somebody else. This is a sign of trouble to come.

Red Flag 7: The Contractor Doesn't Offer a Written Guarantee. This can be tricky because most small contractors work on many different types of construction projects and do not have a standard written guarantee. If it is only a small project and a reputable source gave you the contractor's contact info, you will probably be fine. But if it is a large, expensive job, demand a written guarantee. Better safe than sorry.

Red Flag 8: The Contractor Refuses to Sign a Written Contract. If you don't have your agreements in writing, you get what you deserve. I keep a carbonless statement book in my truck at all times. When a contractor and I agree on a job, I don't leave it to chance. I write it down in the statement book and have him sign it. We both get a copy in case there is a dispute.

Red Flag 9: Unsolicited Home Improvement Financing Offers. When a contractor offers to finance a project, remember that he will make money from the interest on the loan. Sometimes, it will be more than he makes on the project. If you cannot get financing on your own, or you cannot afford to pay cash for the job, do yourself a favor and wait until you can.

Red Flag 10: The Contractor is Not Licensed and Insured. Before you sign a contract, make sure the contractor provides you a copy of his state license, worker's compensation records, and liability insurance policy. Hopefully, nobody will be injured on your property, but if they are, and you do not have those documents, you may have a hard time protecting yourself in court.

Red Flag 11: The Contractor Uses Pressure or Scare Tactics. If a contractor says, "I can tell your roof is going to start leaking the next time a big rain storm hits," or "The price of lumber is going to increase next week," your ears should perk up and you should look for someone else.

Red Flag 12: The Contractor Doesn't Have Local References. Let me make this perfectly clear: no contractor is ever going to give you negative references. If he cannot provide any local references that tells you all you need to know.

Red Flag 13: The Contractor Offers a Great Price Only Good for Today. If a contractor or salesperson says he is offering a discount only good for today, pass on the offer. It is a sign of desperation, and it's not good to do business with desperate people.

Red Flags & Scams

SCAMS

Scam 1: The Contractor Doesn't Do Anything After Being Paid a Large Down Payment. This might be the number one construction scam. If this happens to you, report it to the police, the state attorney general, and any other agency that regulates the construction industry.

Many honest, hardworking contractors will ask for reasonable down payments before they start working. A few highly unscrupulous individuals travel around the country regularly pulling off this scam. They go from town to town and try to get a few people to give them large down payments. They leave town as soon as they have the money. These con artists are almost impossible for the police to identify and catch. They do not leave behind any form of identification or contact information, other than the local telephone number they used, which is usually disconnected by the time the police are called.

Scam 2: Storm Scams. Whenever a large storm devastates a community, hundreds of contractors rush there looking for work. They know insurance companies will pay out billions of dollars in claims and that the local residents desperately need their homes repaired.

Whenever people have roofs ripped off their homes, they are in a very vulnerable position and may make poor decisions. They are easy targets and are more prone to being scammed. If you ever find yourself in this position, do not take any shortcuts, no matter how bad your situation may be.

Hiring Contractors

Scam 3: Roofing Scams. This is an easy one for a contractor to pull off. The contractor doesn't replace the roof he was hired to do. It won't be obvious until after the next storm, by which time the contractor will be long gone.

How many homeowners are going to climb up a ladder to make sure that a roofing job was done correctly? If they do, will they know what they are looking at?

Finding and repairing a leaking roof is difficult, even for an honest and experienced roofing contractor. A roof leak can appear to be coming from one place, when the damage is actually on another part of the roof. Do your due diligence and you won't fall victim to this scam.

Scam 4: The Driveway Sealing Scam. The only thing good about this scam is that it won't cost you much money. This scam starts with somebody knocking at your door and telling you he just sealed a driveway around the corner. He has some materials left over and will do your driveway for next to nothing.

If he actually uses sealer, which in most cases is doubtful, it will be watered down and won't last very long. If somebody approaches you with materials left over from another job, pass, no matter how good of a deal it may seem.

Scam 5: Unlicensed Locksmiths. What could possibly be worse than locking yourself outside and calling a locksmith, only for him to get halfway through the job and tell you it is going to cost you three times as much as his original quote?

If you need to use a locksmith, make sure he is licensed. This is the only way to make sure you are protected.

Scam 6: Paid Material Receipts and Lien Waivers. This scam is usually only perpetrated by somewhat legitimate contractors. Whenever a contractor works on your home, he has the right to put a lien on it until the bill is paid off.

Part of what makes this scam successful is the only way you find out that you are a victim is when you go to sell your home and discover there is a lien on it. In order to protect yourself, ask for material receipts and lien waivers while the job is taking place.

Scam 7: Misrepresentation of Materials. This is a typical construction scam most people would not be able to identify if they were looking right at it. In some areas of the country, plywood is used as a subsurface material for roofs. The building codes that control the thickness of plywood vary by location. For example, in Florida, where they have to protect against hurricanes, the plywood used on roofs is much thicker than the plywood used in Oklahoma.

If a contractor wants to save money and make a job more profitable, he will undercut the prices of other bidders by using a lighter grade of plywood than what is required.

How can you protect yourself? Ask as many questions as you can think of, understand the work that has to be done before you hire a contractor, only employ licensed and insured contractors, and inspect the work daily.

Hiring Contractors

Scam 8: Payment Schedules That Do Not Leave You Fully Protected. Some contractors will try to negotiate payment schedules that require them to be paid in full before the job is complete.

Never, ever fall for this scam. Most contractors will ask for a deposit, which is fine. If the job is going to take more than a few weeks to finish, they might also require for partial payments to be made over the life of the job. This is standard operating procedure in the construction industry, and you should not be concerned about. Contractors have to pay their crews and they have overhead.

When you pay for a job before it is 100 percent complete, you are giving up your leverage, and unscrupulous contractors know this. No reputable contractor will put you in this situation. No matter how good of a deal you might think you are getting, if the payment schedule requires that the work be paid for before everything is finished walk away and find somebody else.

Scam 9: Green Deals Proposed by Salespeople. In certain places, utility companies or city and state governments are offering rebates if you install green devices that reduce your home's power consumption.

A typical offer could be a $5,000 rebate when you install a set of $20,000 solar panels that will decrease your electric bill by up to 25 percent. That offer is legit, and should be utilized if you can afford it. What is not legit is when a salesperson approaches you about the offer, and then requests a $500 processing fee.

Companies that install solar panels or any green energy-saving devices know what kind of rebates their customers are entitled to, and will never ask for a processing fee in order for you to receive what is rightfully yours.

Scam 10: Free Home Inspections. One hundred percent of the time, a company that offers a free home inspection is going to find something that needs to be repaired. Reliable and trustworthy companies do not travel around neighborhoods providing free home inspections. They are far too busy on other projects.

Scam 11: The Contractor Offers Free TVs or Other Gadgets to the Next Person Who Signs Up for a Job. Nothing in life is free. If you are contacted by a contractor who states every customer who signs a contact this week will receive a free TV, remember you are paying for that television set. As soon as the word "free" comes out of a contractor or salesperson's mouth, do yourself a favor and walk away as quickly as possible.

Scam 12: The Contractor Performs More Work Than His Bid Described. If a contractor comes to you after a job is finished and tells you it required more work than expected and he needs to charge you twice as much as his bid, put your checkbook back in your pocket and find the nearest exit. Then pull out the detailed estimate he gave you before the project started and refuse to pay any amount over that unless the contractor can justify the increase.

SPOKEN LIKE A PRO

"The world doesn't want excuses, just answers and solutions."

-Devin Long

If you read *The Savvy Landlord*, you know I think interviews are a great way to learn. If you understand what other people have gone through and learn from their failures and successes, you can avoid many of the pitfalls that keep people from building wealth.

One of the quickest and easiest ways to build your empire is to learn from investors who have dealt with contractors in the past. You can learn more in an hour by talking to someone who has gone before you than you can in months of slugging it out on your own. I spoke with the people below to give you more tools to help you choose the right contractors and team members. Be savvy. Learn from the interviews that follow and hire the right people.

Trusted Handyman

Here are some words of wisdom from my trusted handyman, Devin Long. We have been working together as team for several years. He is a contractor, and I am an investor.

Tell us about your background. How did you become so handy? Did someone teach you or were you born great?

I grew up around a lot of different contractors, bricklayers, builders, and people who were just naturally handy. I picked up skills from them, including the basics such as how to measure a piece of wood. I could jump out there and lay bricks on a house.

I come from a family of bricklayers and it was just natural to learn how to be handy. I've also spent the last decade in construction. Using my hands became natural to me.

Do you enjoy contracting?

I enjoy certain aspects of it depending on the project. I like to start. I like to design. I like to put ideas in motion and guide other people to finish the project.

Put on your contractor's hat. What's the process? If someone calls you and says, "I need a new kitchen," what's the first thing that comes to your mind? Is it price or how to get the job done?

The first thing I will do is to start asking questions. I'm going to ask to see the project firsthand because I don't like surprises. I like to know what I'm dealing with ahead of time. Then I'm going to try to get a face-to-face with them and get off the phone because sometimes you can get stung without knowing all the details.

So you would never quote a price over the phone?

I will try not to. I might give a range.

As a contractor, what's the first thing you think of when you are approached about a project?

I ask if I can do it. Is it possible? There is a sense of excitement if you know you can do it because it's a new project and every home is different. It's a different experience for every house you work in. There's a bit of excitement because you're helping these customers with their design, their dream, their image of their kitchen they see. It's exciting helping them with the growing process.

How do you bid a job? What goes through your mind when you are trying to set a price?

I look at a couple of different things. How extensive is the job? How long is it going to take? How easy is it going to be to get equipment and supplies in and out? How many hours is it going to take? What tools and supplies will I need?

Do you prefer for customers to purchase material or do you buy them and then charge the customer?

I would prefer for them to get the materials. That way, I do not have to worry about it. It saves me time because they're picking it up and bringing it back. It allows them to pick out what they want as opposed to me guessing and hoping that I grab the right thing. That also prevents them from pointing the finger at me if they don't like it later.

You have a choice. You can do a job for a retail customer and charge $1,000 or do the same job for a landlord and charge $500. Who would you prefer to work with and why?

Probably landlords because they're easier to deal with than customers on an actual retail job. Retail customers have different expectations than landlords. Landlords want to save money so the priority is normally to get the work done as quickly as possible. It's a quicker payday.

How about the quality? Is it the same quality?

Pretty much. You can make $500 more with retail customers but it might not be worth the headache, especially if they occupy the home that you're trying to work on. You might have to work around their schedules. You have to work around their furniture. You have to work around their kids and their dogs. You have obstacles you generally don't have with landlords. If you're remodeling their kitchen and they need to cook something you might get relegated to one part of the kitchen and you won't have the whole room to work in anymore. Plus, with landlords, there is the possibility you may get multiple jobs over a period of time and that landlord may talk to other landlords.

What happens when you get to a job site and some of it is out of your scope? Do you dive in and try to do it? Do you try to outsource it?

I would research it to see if I could possibly even learn it and then if I determine that I can, then I learn it and I do. If it's out of my scope, then

I pass it off. I just get it done without telling the customer because I want them to maintain confidence in me.

What's one tip you would love to pass along?

Don't take long on a property that's occupied. On one project, I was dealing with an investor, and I was also dealing with a lady tenant in an unfinished property. She had expectations, she wanted this and this and this and I knew that the landlord only wanted this and this and this. It was difficult trying to find an in between that would satisfy both the landlord's budget and tenant's expectations.

I've learned that lesson. If you're rehabbing a house from start to finish, have it finished before moving someone in. It causes so much trouble moving around couches, painting, and then it's never up to their expectation. People are all nice until they move in.

Have you ever been on a job site as the point person when another contractor shows up on the site because the investor decided the project was behind schedule? How do you handle that?

Yes, that has happened. I wouldn't play that game. I may talk with the customer or have a talk with the investor to determine boundaries. I need to know who's the chief, who's the Indian, who's in charge of what portion of the project. Maybe we need to split up the job load, the new guy takes on bedrooms or whatever and I continue on with the kitchen and bathroom. I ask, "How are we going to split up the work?"

When you are hiring workers, do you prefer them to be specialized or individuals who can do everything?

Well, there are pros and cons on both sides. If you're dealing with specialized contractors, like a plumber or an electrician, the pros are that if you ever get inspected, more than likely it will be done per code. But they are a bit pricier. If you're dealing with someone who's experienced in everything, not necessarily a master of any one specific thing, you're going to save on the cost up front, but it may not be cheaper in the long run because the work may not meet state codes.

What qualities do you look for in a contractor?

Well, price is one, obviously. And knowledge is important. I want to see how much they know. Are they going to try to sell me? Are they the car salesman type? Are they trying to upsell? Are they trying to tell me more is wrong than what really is wrong? Are they're trying to exaggerate the job? Those are some things I look for. You can usually tell if someone is exaggerating a job, especially if you've interviewed multiple electricians. If the bulk of them have come in at an average of $2,000 and one guy comes in at $7,000, he's probably trying to exaggerate the job.

Tell me about your experience with Craigslist.

I was on a jobsite and needed to hire an electrician. I went through Craigslist, pulled five different numbers from the list and started making calls. I had them all come by the property, take a look at it, and give me an estimate.

Hiring Contractors

Four out of the five came and the investor gave me another phone number. I called that electrician and he came. One of them tried to pull the up sell: "There's more wrong than what you know." He gave a $10,000 bid. The other guys understood all I needed was a meter base repaired. They gave me bids that were close to one another.

I decided to hire an older gentleman. His appearance was impressive. He had a tidy, clean, neat appearance. He talked sincerely and had a genuine approach to the job. He wasn't trying to oversell anything and his price was decent. It wasn't over the top. He may have even come in underneath everybody else. I also remember how organized he was. His vehicle was clean, and his tools were stacked in orderly fashion. I take all of these into consideration when looking at people because if they keep their vehicles and their appearance tidy, more than likely they're going to keep the jobs neat. They are going to make sure everything's buttoned up the right way, and the pipes are going to be cut at the right angles and not just point A to point B. The end the job's going to get done the right way. The best part was the price. He rewired the entire house for $2,000.

What other ways do you use to find contractors or service professionals?

I get referrals from other people in the industry, either landlords or another contractor or another foreman. You can ask family members about people they used for their projects.

Should people hide their valuables from contractors?

Not all contractors are thieves. It depends on the people you're dealing with. Do they give the impression of not being trustworthy?

Should I give contractors a key and allow them to be in a property alone?

If you've worked with them enough and have developed trust, you can. Would you give them a key to your home? If you feel like you can give them a key to your house, then it's okay to give them a key to your properties.

Should you add a timeline or a penalty if a job is not completed on time?

It depends on the situation. You may dive into a job and come across things you didn't know were wrong. You may start pulling up the floor and discover the joints are rotted. That's extra repair added time to the job. If you're going to put in a penalty for going over a certain amount of time, you need to also have the stipulation that gives additional time when needed if something is discovered on the property you couldn't have known about before.

Should you visit the jobsite every day to make sure the work is being done?

For an investor's or landlord's point of view, yes. On the contractor's side, they feel like you're sweating them when you do that.

Hiring Contractors

Any final thoughts you would like to share with our readers?

Pay attention to the people you hire. Look at everything. Look at the way they walk, the way they talk, they way they dress, the way they carry themselves, what they drive, and how they keep their tools in their trucks. Every detail matters.

Seasoned Investor Lady

Here is an interview with an investor who asked to remain anonymous. She has a ton of great experience and works for a large company. She has amazing insight, and you need to take advantage of that.

What is the first thing you would tell investors to do when dealing with contractors or when they decide to rehab a house?

The first thing I would say when rehabbing a house is that you have to decide where you're going to stop, because if you don't, the work will never end. There's always something else you could do. You have to have a budget in terms of time and money.

And you have to understand the market value of the property, because you can't afford to overspend on the project. You can't oversell a house in the neighborhood. We've tried. You should never over-improve in a neighborhood.

Does that mean you should always buy the cheapest house in the neighborhood?

You can't always buy the cheapest, but you never want to buy the most expensive house on the block, either. Somebody has to, but as far as an investment goes, you probably would never want to buy the most expensive house in the neighborhood. If you do that, you may never make your money back. As an investor, I always want to buy the ugliest house on the nicest block.

What would you do differently if you could?

I've made a lot of mistakes in rehabbing, and I think the biggest one was not understanding the importance of communication. You and your contractor have to be on the same page. Because what I think is right may not be what he thinks is right. I'll give you an example. We rehabbed a really cute house on the southwest side of town. It was a short sale. We bought it at the right price. It had hardwood floors, and a master bedroom over the garage. It was as cute as it could be. I painted the door a pretty color and it was beautiful. It had a doormat at the front door. I sold it to a first-time homebuyer, a single girl. She had it inspected, and things started falling apart. Under the kitchen sink, the former owners had cut a Pepsi bottle in half and had used it as a funnel to take the water from the sink drain to the plumbing, and we never noticed it.

No one saw it until the property was inspected. Obviously, from the beginning, our scope was not right because we never opened the cabinets under the sink to see what was there. We ran water, and it looked like the plumbing was functioning properly, but it was a scam. And from there it went downhill. By the time the inspection was done, there were thousands of dollars in repairs. She still bought the property after we made the repairs. But we could have avoided the entire problem if the contractor and I had been on the same page from the start.

What other problems have you dealt with?

Another issue I have seen several times is collapsed sewer lines. You can't dig up an entire line and examine it, so I've started adding, "I don't know" to my disclosures. There really isn't a way to know when you buy an investment property, rehab it, and sell it. I think the line works, but I don't know. I've never done laundry and a load of dishes while my kid was taking a shower, but where I live, sewer lines are not part of the disclosures so I can get away without a complete answer to the question.

A disclosure asks, "To your knowledge, is everything in working order?" Well, to my knowledge, it is, but you're better off putting "unknown" and saying, "Let's have it inspected." I know two investors who have been sued about the sewer lines. After the deals closed, the sewer lines collapsed and the purchasers had plumbers tell them, "You need a new sewer line. It's going to cost $1,500. Go scream bloody murder because you got ripped off." So the sellers had a choice. They could get sued or fix the sewer line.

You have experience in almost every aspect of real estate and have met your fair share of roofers. Anyone who ever owns a house will have to deal with a roofer at some point, and that intimidates a lot of people. How do you deal with roofing contractors?

I've done it a lot of different ways. At one point, I used one roofer exclusively because he did a lot of inspections for me for free. There were houses that I was looking to buy, and I would give him all my roofing business. It worked well for a while until he got really, really busy. Now I try to contract turnkey, and I hire my contractor to be the general contractor, and then he coordinates all of the labor, work, and material. That's a pretty expensive way to get things done. His bid covers his overhead. But with the volume of work that we were doing, if he came up short on one job, he could make it up on another. At the height of my rehabbing, we were doing five or six houses at a time, and the same guy was doing all of them. He worked almost exclusively for me and for himself. He became an investor after he saw how much profit could be made. He even bought a few houses from us and we financed them.

Now that he is more of an investor than a contractor, I am getting at least two bids from roofing companies, and I have one roofing company that I'm starting to work with almost exclusively again.

Suppose your favorite handyman and contractor are busy and you have a house coming down the pipe. You know it's going to be a moneymaker and there's $30,000 on the table. What are the first things that you would do to find a contractor?

All the contractors I have hired have been referrals from someone who used them before and had good success. I'm getting ready to hire a guy to do a rent house for us. We've never met, but he has bid on two or three houses and his bids look fairly decent, so that hire may be more trial and error. As long as he understands from the very beginning what he has to do and what I expect, I think it'll be a successful relationship. But the biggest times I've messed up are when I have not communicated well or I've been so busy that I just said, "Oh, he knows what I want." That was a big mistake. The most money I lost this year was on a house that my contractor and I were going to rehab for a rent-ready landlord.

The fees and the holding costs got big. When we started, we were going to use some old cabinets we found in another house, but when we got them, they looked so bad we bought new cabinets. That was the beginning of the end. We bought new cabinets, then we installed ceiling fans, then we did granite countertops, then we did stainless steel appliances, and I rehabbed a three-bedroom, one-bathroom house, in a rental neighborhood and lost my shirt. We finally sold it to a landlord at a loss. I was so busy last year. I was overwhelmed, and I let that house get away from me. I don't usually lose money on houses that I sell or rehab. We usually make a profit or we wouldn't be doing it as long as we have. But I lost money on that house, because I let the contractor get carried away.

Tell me about a time when you hired someone and it failed.

I hired one contractor I had never used before and I wasn't sure about him. I gave him a small job to see how he would perform. He didn't perform well. I didn't lose money because I didn't let him get away from me. I held my expectations and when it was not where I wanted it to be, I just paid him and sent him on his way.

Here was the first clue. It took him six days to do a half-day job. It took him six days to find the time to do it. Every day he gave me another excuse. "Well, I started a job here, and it's going to take me two days and I only thought it would be one. Sorry." "Well, now I'm somewhere else doing central heat and air, a sub job for this guy, and he subbed it for two days and it's going to take me five."

All the guy had to do was put some trim around a window, and when he finally got around to doing it, he installed it upside down. When I asked him about it, he shrugged his shoulders and said, "I did it upside down, but it doesn't show anywhere else, and it was easier to do it that way." He didn't even have the integrity to make it right.

My boss always says, "You would love to think that you could find a handyman who would be stable, who would be dependable, somebody that you could keep for more than six or nine months." I don't want this to be an indictment of every handyman in the world, but I've come to learn that a lot of people become handymen because they can't respond properly in a work environment.

There are exceptions, but I may be jaded. I can't tell you how many handymen we've had with drug or alcohol problems or girlfriend problems. Their lives are just a mess. I've gone through it so many times that whenever we hire someone new, I give him the same spiel. "If you do a good job, we'll keep you around. You can work for us." But I know the reality is most of them aren't going to. It's the reality of the job, and your readers should know that before they hire people to work on their properties.

Hiring Contractors

Another investor told me the same thing once. If a handyman were so good or worth as much as you're paying, he would be on his own by now, or working with a successful company.

That's right. Some of them have been incarcerated, and the trust factor and my expectations are really low. I can't tell you the number of stories where investors have given a handyman or contractor a $1,200 check only to have him disappear. The guy goes on a bender and disappears for four or five days.

Again, I am not trying to be judgmental. I have been lucky, I have worked hard, and I have my family behind me. But sometimes I want to grab these contractors and say, "Wake up! I could give you so much more work if you would give me the chance." I don't even really have to say that to people. If they don't get it, they're never going to get it. If they come to our office and don't realize that we're a family that has plenty of money and we pay our bills on time, if I have to say that, then they're probably not going to understand it.

Say you get a smoking deal on a house. You think, "I can't go wrong. I'm going to get this rehab going and knock this out of the park." But then you realize you miscalculated and the rehab is going to cost way more than you budgeted and the margins aren't there. How do you determine when it's time to get out?

I can sell anything if the buyer is willing to pay too much and if it has a great location. You can fix a house, you can make it pretty, but you can never improve a house's location. For a big return, you've got to have a location. I'd be willing to increase my rehab budget on a property if the location was right.

Tell me about another experience helping investors with a contractor that wasn't so honest. I know you have a hundred of those.

We bought a house once in a desirable, older part of town. It was a good-looking little house on a corner, and it had a gun safe in the closet. I told my contractor he could have it if he could get it out. He had no clue what I meant. He cut the closet, just cut out the doorframe, left the damage, and took the safe. He never fixed it. It was unbelievable.

Do you pay by the job or by the hour?

By the job. By the hour never works.

Do you try to keep one contractor on one project or do you try to keep him moving in different directions? Do you have anyone that's been with you for a long time?

We have tried everything. We've had contractors, and we've had construction coordinators on staff. If there was a different way of trying things, odds are we did it.

One of our coordinators used to tell his contractors, "Git'r done." He didn't care how things got done, as long as the work was completed. One time we were in his truck and I heard him tell a contractor something.

"What did you just say to him?" I asked.

Hiring Contractors

"Git'r done."

I was a little confused. "Do you know how much he's going to charge you to 'git'r done?'"

"I don't care," he told me.

I said, "That's the problem. You don't care."

"I just need to get it done."

"No, that's not how we do siding. That's not how we do roofs. We don't just get it done. You don't have any idea. You're not in control of your budget at all."

"It doesn't matter." We fired him not long after that.

We hired someone to replace him, and that went well for a while, but it didn't take long for that to fall apart. He wasn't spending his own money, and things got out of control. We went to contractors by the job, and we would hire individuals on 1099s and pay them by the job. We've done that two different ways: we would give them authority to charge on the charge account at Lowe's or we would give them a Lowe's gift card to use. When it was empty, we would load it back up. We finally agreed to meet them and purchase the materials, and then they would go and do the job. That seems to work best for us. I don't have any employees on the account now.

We had a guy who worked for us who bought $2,500 worth of stuff for a house and we didn't recognize the address. We were able to have criminal charges filed against him and Lowe's gave us the money back to us because he wasn't on the account. He used somebody else's name.

Right now I'm contracting with a new handyman service. One of the good things is that I don't have to worry about workmen's comp and the liability is on the company. I pay a higher rate, but it should be worth it in the long run.

How do you do a background check on someone who's going to work for you?

We have them go to the state bureau of investigation and bring us a full criminal report. We reimburse them for it if there are no problems. Then we go to a database online and double check their arrest record and see if there have been any civil cases filed against them. It's free, and it lets us weed out the bad ones.

Any final thoughts that could help a fellow investor?

Years ago, my ex-husband and I were building a house on a lot in a beautiful, gated community. The lot was on the water and on the golf course. We went out there quite a bit on Sundays after lunch. We'd drive out and look at the house as it was being built. One day, I was standing in the place where my kitchen was going to be, and I pointed to a wall. I looked at my ex-husband and asked, "What's that?"

"It's a wall made of concrete block."

"I know, but it's not supposed to be there." We designed this house because it was on the golf course and on the water. The whole room was going to be glass. The doors were going to be stacking sliders to give us a better view.

Hiring Contractors

"You're crazy."

We went home and pulled out the plans. I pointed to where the wall was. "What does SGD stand for?"

"Sliding glass door," and then he realized what I meant.

"There's supposed to be a sliding glass door where that wall is," I told him.

It was a holiday weekend, and I had to wait until Tuesday to call the contractors.

When the contractor looked at the plans and then the wall, he shook his head and muttered, "Well, I'll be damned." They had to tear down the wall.

The moral of the story is, if we had not been in the area - if we had not gone to the house on a regular basis - I would've had a wall where the sliding glass door was supposed to be, and it would've ruined my million-dollar view.

The same thing goes with rehabbing a house. You've got to go to the house, or you may wind up with a wall where it is not supposed to be.

You can't have someone do your work for you without your influence. You can't have someone read your mind on how you want something done. People don't always think alike and you have to make sure your contractor knows exactly what you want done.

That's just the nature of the business. If you want your house to turn out right, you've got to go to the site every day or every other day, and you've got to have the kind of relationship with the contractor where it's not an inconvenience for you to be there. I've had contractors ask, "Why do you have to come out here all the time?"

Because it's my house. Because I'm rehabbing it. Because it's my money. Because I want to make sure that it's being done. You know? I want to make sure that you and I are on the same page.

Greg Meech

I'm honored to know Greg from a Mr. Landlord conference. We were quick and fast friends and hip-to-hip for several days. He has a different perspective of real estate investing in Houston, Texas, and he's doing a great job.

Tell me a little bit about yourself.

I've been in real estate some time, about four and a half years. I only had one property for three years, one that I inherited from my mom. I made a lot of mistakes on that property, but I finally found a way to make a profit on it and decided to expand. I went from one property to nine in a year and a half.

How many times have you hired a contractor?

Too many. I never get a chance to work with the same contractor for some reason. I have probably worked with thirty or forty contractors over the last four years.

Can you tell us about an experience with a contractor that you wish you'd never endured?

Unfortunately, yes. At the beginning of my investing career, I got one of

Hiring Contractors

my first properties in Houston. I hooked up with the local REIA group. Before I became a full-time investor, I didn't know there were such things as real estate clubs. I took the advice of the real estate club in Houston and used their contacts. I got contacts for contractors, banks, and management companies. There were a lot of vendors trying to get our work. I was led to believe the contractors were pre-screened and had worked with other investors.

I got a contractor's name from one of the members of the real estate club. The people in the group are professionals, the kind of people I want to be when I grow up. I aspire to own fifty properties, and I thought they could help me get there. Some of them owned ten properties, and I only had one. I knew there was no need to reinvent the wheel, so I thought I would follow in their footsteps. They told me, "Use this contractor. These guys are good. They're investor-friendly," which, if you don't know, is a term for cheap.

I called this guy up and I told him I bought my first house, and I need to rehab it. "We can do that." He came out and gave an estimate. Not being the smartest guy, I trusted him. I just wanted to work with this guy because the investors in the club told me he was good. I told that guy I'd give him all the work on the property.

He quoted me a fee of $11,000 and told me he needed half the money up front to buy materials and supplies and pay his crew. That sounded reasonable so I gave him a check for $6,000, and he told me the work would take about three and a half weeks.

He went to work, brought his guys there, started pounding, and made a bunch of noise. It looked great to me, so I went back to my day job. A couple of days later I came back about 11:00 in the morning and no one was there. I called him and left a voicemail. "I need you guys out here. I need you guys to get this work done." I looked around the jobsite again and saw a few beer cans, a ladder, and a bunch of material. I didn't see any work being done. I came back the next day and nothing had been touched. I started leaving more aggressive messages on the contractor's phone.

I never saw the contractor again. I now have a $6,000 ladder sitting in my garage. That was the only thing I got out of the deal.

This contractor was supposed to do everything. He was supposedly approved by the real estate club. Because I respected and admired those guys, I didn't have my guard up. The big mistake I made was giving him the control by handing over so much money at the start of the project.

Once I gave him the money, I'm sure he found another job that was more important or was just too busy getting drunk or whatever. I wound up hiring another contractor to get the work done. It cost me $6,000 out of pocket, a couple of days' worth of work, and a ton of stress.

The moral is that the person who has the money has the control. Don't give the control to a contractor too early because you're the one who has everything to lose.

How did you rebound from that?

At the time, I owned the property and had very few choices. It cost me a lot of money every day. When you face challenges like that, you can give up and try to sell the property, or you can complete it. I don't give up. I took a step back and tried to look at the big picture. I learned that I had to accept the mistake. I had two choices. I could give up. I could have had the mindset that this house wasn't going to work out and I could have been done with real estate. I had to get the house out of my name and sell it or finish it.

I went the other way. I finished the project, just hired another contractor and did a lot of the work myself while the contractor was there. From that point forward, I was scared. I would only pay contractors when they were done. I stayed onsite, doing the work myself because budget was pretty constrained.

Once it was all done, I still made money on the deal. I said to myself, "It was my first house and I didn't get the right deal on it. I paid too much for it, it wasn't in the right area, I didn't hire the right contractor, it wasn't done on time and it went over budget. At the end, I still made a profit. A small one, but it was still a profit. Damn! What if I actually knew how to do this right? I could really make a successful living out of this." I knew I was in a learning curve and could learn from each deal I did and would start making fewer mistakes. At the end of each rehab, I decided to reevaluate my decisions. "I could have done that a little faster. I could get a better deal on that. I can use different materials on the next project." I try to learn from every single house.

Spoken Like A Pro

How do you approach it now? What do you do differently?

I had to change how I thought about making money with real estate. I have a full-time day job. It takes up to forty hours a week, so I'm not looking for cash flow from my real estate. I'm looking for equity. If you use real estate to create cash flow, you have to go to it every single day as much as you can. I don't have to do that because I'm thinking about long-term equity. In a couple of years, my properties will be worth a lot. I may not get cash flow off of it right now, but the properties are going to have more equity at the end, and that's when I will flip the property and cash out big time.

When I got into real estate, I was looking for an investment where I would get a return that was better than Bank of America's 21 percent annual return on the stock market. You're always risking the principal in the market, and nothing is in your control.

I used conventional loans when I started buying properties. I didn't do any of the special "no money down" deals. I went to the bank and said, "I want to get a second house." They said, "You need to put 20 percent down." I put 20 percent down and figured what my return would be. You always need to crunch the numbers because maybe it's not going to be a good deal. Maybe it's a better deal to buy an oil well. Maybe it's better to put your money in the stock market or to buy gold and silver.

I looked at real estate ads and decided buying property was the best place to invest my money with the safest return and the highest return. That's actually why I got into real estate. Not the cash flow, not for equity, but for the highest return of my money without risking my principal. The bonus was, I got equity and I got cash flow. But that's not why I got into it.

You need contractors to keep it going because you have a full-time job. What advice would you give someone who needs to hire a contractor? How do you pre-screen them?

It's hard. The best way to screen a contractor is if he comes with a recommendation. But then you have to screen the person who gave the recommendation. If a real estate club tells you, "Oh, this guy is great," he may have an interest in the club or maybe he paid for that recommendation. Find an actual investor that has actually used the contractor before. You can call up other investors and say, "Hey, do you know anybody who can clean properties and anybody who can do tile?" That's one way I screen. I get other people who say they've used him in the past. But I still only hire about 50 percent of contractors with good references because particular contractors who are great for me may be terrible for someone else. There are many reasons for that. I may be on the north side of town, but the contractor is on the south side of town. It's just not worth his time. I may have a small job and the other guy has a big job. I may only use him once every six months in the town, but someone else is using him for all kinds of things.

It's also important that a contractor is easy to get in touch with. If I can't get in touch with one, he's not going to work out for me. Other investors may not care. They just come at the last minute and see if the job's done.

Spoken Like A Pro

Good recommendations are not the Holy Grail. They are just one way. You still have to be very skeptical. I also use Craigslist a lot, but you have to realize Craigslist has a lot of bad people on it.

If I was going to hire an employee, I could spend a lot of time to interview him. When you hire a contractor, you don't get any of that. You don't get to see a résumé. You don't get to see a clear-cut value. You don't get to see a guy that even has a phone number that rings in an office. It's a different class of people. Unless you're going to get a company that's very big and very expensive, which you're not going to be able to use on one or two smaller properties, you have to deal with a contractor like the guys you find on Craigslist.

It doesn't really matter what they say. Their actions speak louder than words. My interview starts the moment I call them on the phone. I usually get upset when you call their cellphones and they don't answer. When they answer, I say something like, "Hey, I found you on Craigslist. Do you do roofs?" "Yes, we do roofs."

I try to find out if this contractor specializes in one thing or if he does everything. That's actually pretty important, because if he says he does everything, he can't do it all himself. He has to hire it out to some other people. He has friends who will do it. If he does everything, you'll hire a general contractor, which is a completely separate category.

Then you need to decide if you want to hire a general contractor and have him get all the subs for you. It's going to cost a little more, but it's

Hiring Contractors

going to be less headache as long as you get a good contractor. Or do you want to hire the individual subs and be your own general contractor? You have to decide what path you want to go on. If you got a big house, a lot of work, and you don't want to be there, you can pay extra and you can hire a general contractor. He's going to hire the painter. He's going to hire the foreman. He's going to hire the floor guy and then put it all together for you. He'll be one point contact that you can talk to, and that makes it easier on you. But it's going to cost you a little more, probably an average of 20 or 25 percent more.

It depends on what's more important for you - your time or your money. If you have extra money but you don't have a lot of time, you may want to hire a general contractor and let him go through the hassle of dealing with Jose being the painter and Bob being the plumber and another guy being the electrician. When you start off, money's pretty tight. If you have time, it's probably not a bad idea to be your own general contractor for a couple of reasons. You can get a better price, and you can micro-manage the job and make sure it's done the way you want in the time frame you want. Plus, you're going to learn a lot about it. If you don't know anything about plumbing or flooring, it's hard to tell what a good deal is. I decided pretty early on, being a micromanaging kind of guy, I wanted to weed out all the general contractors and deal directly with the guy doing the work.

You also need to ask who will be doing the work. I had a painter give me a quote. At least I thought he was a painter because he had paint all over his shirt and a paint truck. I never saw him after he gave me the bid. He hired this cousin or his daughter to come paint the house, and he went and got another bid. Find out who's going to be doing the work.

Another great technique I learned is to ask the right questions on the phone to make sure you and the contractor are on the same page. If I'm looking for a painter, I don't want to waste their time and my time, because everybody wastes time getting a bid. I try to give them as much information as they would need. I put myself in their shoes. If I bid on the house that I'm looking at right now, what would I do? I would tell him, "I have a thousand-square-foot house. It's textured. I just need primer and paint. What would you charge me for that?" "That'd be $5,000." Depending on your budget, he may have priced himself out of the job. But if he says, "I don't know. I really prefer to see it, but it might be $1,500," that might be a guy you would meet.

When you talk to him, you can find out if he's a general contractor or if he does the work himself. I always ask, "What do you charge per square foot to paint a house?" The good ones will say something like, "It's, on average, a dollar a square foot, but there's textures. There are high ceilings. A lot of factors impact the price." When he says something like that, it's obvious the guy knows what he's talking about. I always try to get him to give me a quote on the phone, because if he's experienced and he's done it a hundred times, he already knows what it's going to take.

If he has no idea, it means one of two things. He hasn't done it enough, or he's getting calls and having someone else do the work. They don't want to turn down any work, so they'll have their friend or cousin or co-worker do it, and they'll just tack on a little extra fee. He's a middleman. I pre-screen them on the phone and don't want any middlemen.

Do you have a price in mind when you call someone?

Of course. You have to know how much it's going to cost to repair a house before you buy it. You should itemize it all. When you talk to contractors, they want to do everything. I say no. I give them one specific job. I don't let them have everything. I have multiple contractors at a time.

If a project cost more than I think it should, I need to know why. I make them educate me. I look at my receipts on jobs I paid for in the past and call around to get different quotes. I am not going to pay more than I think I should simply because a contractor tells me to. Obviously, some contractors know more than I do. But if a project goes over my budget, I need to understand why before I write a check.

If the estimate doesn't come in within the ballpark, I need to find out why. One of us is wrong. You've got to have a budget in mind, which requires some work on your part. You have to know a little bit about tiling, a little bit about woodworking, a little bit about painting, and so forth. If you have no clue and you have to ask, "How much does it cost to put tile in?" you won't know if he's overcharging or undercharging. You have to educate yourself either on the Internet or ask other contractors and come up with your budget.

You were green when you started as an investor. How did you learn this stuff?

There are a lot of sources out there, but the biggest and the best one is YouTube. If you want to learn how to do anything, just click on YouTube. There are tons and tons of videos teaching you how to do everything. Say you want to learn how to install baseboards and you don't know how hard it is to put up baseboards. Go to YouTube, type in a search "how to replace baseboards," and you might get 500 links. You click on a few videos. You watch the guy do it. You say, "Oh, wow! That's all you have to do? You just put the caulk on the top and then you take a little pry bar and then gently just pull of this baseboard? It's not too hard."

I can use a handyman at $10 or $15 an hour and some labor to rip up baseboard - just semi-skilled labor. The skill is putting it on, not taking it off, and that's one of the things I learned on YouTube. If you're trying to get the best price, then you have to manage contractors a little bit. When they install baseboard, they talk about how long it takes to cut it and the different sizes. You can become very knowledgeable with a few clicks of your mouse. It's not uncommon for a contractor to come out and start working and I look at his work and say, "Hey, hey. You need to caulk better. Aren't you supposed to put some spray foam in there?" I had one of them look at me and say, "Yes, but I don't have it right now." "Well, stop. I will buy you a $5 can. Let's do it right."

If you spend a little time on YouTube, you may know more than your contractor does. You can learn a lot of techniques online. The videos are right in your face. You could watch a hundred videos online. I recently learned how to replace a circuit breaker in an electrical panel from YouTube, and I didn't know anything about it when I started. I was at a house and the electrical sockets were not working. I went to the panel and I saw that it was dead. I went to YouTube on my phone and typed in "replace circuit breaker panel". There was a five-minute video I watched while I was sitting there. I went out to the panel, turned it off, pulled the thing out, and went to Home Depot and found a replacement. I made sure I used the same model and popped it in. It worked perfectly. Wow! I'm an electrician now! You may not want to do it personally, but it worked for me that time.

How much did you save on that repair?

A cheap electrician would have cost at least $75, and a more expensive one would have run $150. If you're not comfortable doing stuff like that, then don't do it. Hire contractors. You don't have to do the work yourself, but you have to know what they do. You need to know what the problem is when your circuit panel's bad and how much it should cost to replace it. That way, you will know whether his bid is a rip-off or the real cost. You don't want to be in the position where you have to think, "That's electricity. I'm scared. I'm not going to touch it. Whatever you charge, I'm going to pay." You're always going to leave the money on the table if you do that.

Here's another example. I got a great deal on a house, but one of the sprinkler heads wasn't working. I don't know anything about sprinklers. I call a sprinkler guy, he turns up, looks at it, and puts a price on it. He starts doing some work and does a terrible job. I throw him off the property. I'm sitting there and, looking at the broken sprinkler, not knowing what to do. Before I hired anybody else, I went on YouTube and typed in "how to replace a sprinkler head." I found two videos and watched them for the next ten or fifteen minutes while I ate my lunch. I grabbed a Phillips head screwdriver, put it in there, pulled the sprinkler head out, and I typed in "irrigation supply" on my phone. It showed me there was a supply house less than two miles away. There was even a link to a map and the option to call them. I clicked on the phone number and asked if they had the part in stock. They did and I asked how much it was. "$6.22."

"Thank you, sir. I'll be right there." The guy who quoted me before said $60 for the sprinkler head and $120 for labor. Within thirty minutes, I replaced the sprinkler head and saved a ton of money.

The knowledge I learned from YouTube empowered me and made me feel like I was in control.

What else have you learned about contractors?

Contractors are terrible at estimates. Here's typically what happens to a contractor. He gets in with the deal, gives you an estimate, and then starts doing the job. If he doesn't have much experience, somewhere along the way, he thinks, "I totally blew that estimate. I didn't charge enough. I feel like I'm working for free." I had one contractor who had to send his two guys home and pay them himself because he bid so low that he ended up working for $5 an hour to finish the job. They tend to do that and then they feel like they got burned. They are so afraid of getting screwed again they are going to overcharge. Not that he's trying to rip you off. He just doesn't know how to give an estimate. He's terrible at it even estimating time. They're just not good at estimating.

One of the first things I do when I get an estimate is to break down the bill between labor and material. I negotiate on both items separately, because if you throw labor and materials in one big lump sum, you don't know what material you're paying for. When you break them out, materials are going to be priced on the kind of material you choose. After you specify the materials, it comes down to labor. To make it a little easier for contractors, you kind of do the estimates for them. You should explain how long it will take to make them feel more comfortable.

I would actually prefer to pay by the hour, but it doesn't seem to work. If I could get big enough, I would like to hire an employee. If the guy was working only for me, I think I could get my work done at a better price. But that hasn't worked out for me yet. I'm not big enough and don't have enough work to keep someone busy all the time. I believe in the future, I could do that. I have to pay per job for now.

When you pay per job, put your agreement in writing and spell out exactly what your terms are. Make sure you agree on quality, material, time frame, and payment. That's how 99 percent of all landlords do it when they hire someone, and the other 1 percent are making a mistake.

Once you've found someone to work for you, always give him a small job to start with. A hundred interviews aren't as valuable as them doing one job for you. You can see their work, and you can see when they screw up. You can see if they show up at 9:00 a.m. or if they show up at noon, and you can see when they leave. You can see when they show up drunk, you can see when they have materials, and what kind of mess they make. You can see all that. Let them know, "I have ten properties. I need a good tile guy. I don't have one. Is that you? If you do a good job for me, do a good job at a good price I'll give you more work. I'll give you all my tile jobs. I'll put your name up at the real estate club and give you more work." You let them know that this isn't just one time project but a way to make full-time weekly pay from me and from my fellow investor friends. I have more work for you. I can keep your plate full for another few months. You can use me as a reference." He'll do a better job for you.

Roofing Contractor

Here is some input form a contractor's point of view. Ben Shrewsberry has been a roofing contractor for nearly two decades. He has graciously agreed to be interviewed and to share his insight.

Tell us about your company and what you've been doing in real estate.

I have been in the construction industry for about fifteen years. I started as a framer, and now I am a general contractor. I literally started at the ground floor and figured out that there are a lot of different things that make this system work, including lenders and different kinds of contractors. I have spent a lot of time educating myself on how to do each section the best I can. My company has been around for roughly forty-four years.

I have been in the financial service sector of the industry since 2004 as a mortgage broker/lender.

What's the best way for you to get new clients?

Word of mouth is the best referral, but the best-paid advertisements are the Multi-unit Apartment Associations that exist here in the OKC metro. Several people have hired me through the Asian-American Hotel Owners Association.

Walk me through a process. Suppose I'm a new investor, and I need to get my first roof done. What questions should I ask a roofing contractor?

The first thing I would want to know is if they actually have genuine insurance to be a roofer. Almost 90 percent of all roofers out there are running around with insurance for a sheetrock contractor because it's cheaper than buying actual insurance that designates them as a roofer or a roofing contractor. That's the number one safeguard. The second thing is to make sure they actually have worker's compensation insurance that is adequate for the job they are doing. It's more dangerous for you than it is as the contractor to have somebody get hurt on your property.

If someone falls off that roof, they are going to come after you, the property owner, for any lack in insurance. If the contractor is underinsured, they are coming against the property owner. They are not coming after that company.

What questions should a contractor ask a real estate investor who needs a new roof?

The first thing I am going to ask you is whether the work is insurance related or is it due to a leak? We will also discuss whether it needs to be a full replacement or if it's a partial.

What's the process from there?

Whenever people are bidding for work, you are not just bidding for dollars, even though that's what a lot of people ultimately make up their minds based on. Dollars aren't the only side of the presentation that you need to be aware of. Materials are huge in the investment property community because some people use factory seconds and irregulars to save money when the shingles look like they are correct.

If you want to compare contractors, give multiple contractors the same scope of work, which means the same measurement guidelines. It doesn't mean if it's an insurance claim you have to give them the exact bid, but you do have to have each person comparing the same thing. Each person is going to give you a separate number for a different result. That's where I see a lot of investors fall short, because they don't actually compare apples to apples. They don't compare the shingle types, such as twenty-five-year, thirty-year, impact-resistant, or a class four shingle, which is an impact-resistant shingle. The wind ratings aren't even the same on different types of shingles. You need to be specific on the things you want or you won't be happy in the long run.

In order to pick out a contractor, you have to know about the company. Do they normally operate in this area? Have they been in the area for a long time or are they temporary or seasonal, like storm chasing people? Will they be there for a warranty or for a repair claim after the fact? If something were to happen, how is that roof going to be covered after the fact? It's not just putting it on as cheaply as possible. It's who is going to be here for the long haul to actually take care of you.

I have put on several roofs, and there always seems to be extreme differences in pricing. Why is that?

I will go back to insurance every single time because insurance drives a lot of price, for the most part. Many roofers do not have proper insurance, especially for steep charge roofs or things like that. There are a lot of OSHA regulations to follow for harnessing on certain roofs, but that's another conversation.

The liability is on both the contractor and on the property owner when someone is on the roof. Most of the time, the companies that undercut price so severely did not pay for the appropriate insurance.

Is the risk worth the cost of getting a cheaper price? That's why the handyman poses a threat to the investment owner because he is trying to work with a small margin. You might get away with it this time and you might get away with it next time when an uninsured or underinsured person doesn't get harmed on the job site. But when it does happen to you, you can start losing your empire.

A lot of my readers say that when they contact a roofer, a salesman comes out, but he's not involved with the actual work. Is that common?

It's pretty common. The salesmen aren't usually roofers. The salesman is required to have a direct knowledge of the roof systems and how the roof works and what happens, but another person will also come back, which would be the project manager or the job site foreman, and administer the job. In our company, the salesman is the job site foreman. Whoever sold you that job will be on the job site managing and ensuring that what was offered and promised is delivered. I can say that for our company. Not every company does it that way.

A lot of companies come out and put on a good show. They sign you up and send some subcontractors out from their company, but the salesmen never see the roof again. All they cared about was signing the contract, getting your money, and leaving.

How do you find people to work for you? Are they employees or subcontractors?

We have both in-house and subcontracted crews. Our subcontractors have worked for us for years and they carry their own insurance policy in addition to our policy. We carry worker's compensation and general liability, and there is an additional general liability policy on their side. We have double the coverage whenever you enter that situation with our subcontractors. We have our own full-time crews who work for us year round and whenever we get busy in peak season, we have guys who have worked for us for the last decade and we don't ever have to pick up anybody else because our name is already out there. I have a backlog of people who are waiting to work for us if we ever lose the guys who work for us now. It's based on treating people well and having them enjoy doing business with you over time.

What do people not understand about the work roofing contractors do?

People don't realize we negotiate claims to get insurance companies to pay the maximum amount possible. The insurance company's job is to save the company money and to pay the lowest amount. Claims adjustors come out and have no idea what line items should be on claims most of the time, especially when it involves the roof system, what has been damaged underneath, suffered cosmetic damage, or was rough construction.

Our job is to go through adjustment reports. We examine the summaries line by line. I am a licensed insurance professional as well as a contractor, so I understand how those reports are written. I can go through an adjustor's summary report and see the holes in it. Essentially, I am adjusting your claim again to ensure you've gotten what you deserve.

But once I save people money, more times than not, many property owners want to start cutting corners. When we get them several thousand dollars they weren't going to have before, they get greedy. They want to put that in their pocket and they want me to work for nothing, when I'm the one who brought it to the table. That would be my biggest complaint whenever it comes to dealing with investors. They think they are the only ones who deserve to make money.

The other thing is that we always eat the deductible, no matter what it is. On hotels, they are usually $20,000 to $25,000. That's money that the insurer is not spending, so if we get additional money by supplementing the claim, contractors expect to get the full amount of the claim if we are eating the deductible.

How can real estate investors save money when they hire a roofer?

Investors with multiple properties have a built-in advantage. We would take a low-margin deal any day of the week if we knew the investors were going to continue to do business with us. If you have used a contractor on several projects and then give a project to someone else, if we lose the bid, the investor should tell the first contractor why. Was the quality of workmanship not there or should the contract have been re-negotiated? By telling the contractor why you went with someone else, you would be doing us a favor. Plus, any contractor would entertain the ongoing work, especially in the slow season because it's not always storm season in the roofing business.

If you do business with the same contractor, he would be happy to fix roof leaks and repairs and things that come up. That's the relationship that we would like to build when we give you a low, fair price.

Explain worker's comp. Do I need to worry about worker's comp as an investor?

Worker's comp is insurance for wages lost in the event of injury. It covers employees. As an investor, you don't need to be worried about worker's comp. You need to be worried about liability under the umbrella for that person who could be injured on your property. Worker's compensation is only for the employer, not for the contracted. Every contractor should carry proof of worker's comp in his vehicle. You should ask to see it, and they are required to provide a copy of it to you if you would like to have it.

What are some of the roofing scams you've heard of?

The number one scam is when a contractor asks to be paid up front. Never do business with anyone who needs to be paid up front. I have seen too many people come in from out of town, collect insurance checks, and leave good people without roofs on their homes. If someone does request up front money, the maximum you should pay is 50 percent, and that's only after the materials are delivered on site. The average roof is only going to take two days anyways, maximum.

Our guys can do roughly fifty squares a day per eight men. There aren't many roofs that are over fifty squares in a standard neighborhood. That means most roofs should take two days.

Be leery of anyone who doesn't want to work with a mortgage company. Mortgage companies have to sign off on checks. They send an initial check and then they send what is called the recovered depreciation check after the completion report is done. Some people try to send in a completion report to get all their funds so they don't have to wait. You won't have this problem if you hire a successful business that has established credit lines with banks or the required capital to run their business and pay their crews appropriately. Never pay someone until the job is done, but whenever the job is complete, full payment is expected to be rendered.

We are a long-standing company with a good reputation, and many of our customers get their insurance checks and let us handle the entire claims process for them. They essentially endorse the back of their checks, hand them over, and we put their roof on. These customers are comfortable doing that because we have worked with them in the past. That's an exception. You should never give someone a check and sign a contract. That person would more than likely run away with your money.

Suppose you have already quoted a price and then you find damage to the decking. How do you handle that?

It's very common. If it's an insurance claim, it's never a problem because all we have to do is take pictures, document it, and replace it. You can't leave the roof exposed in order to argue with an insurance company. We then supplement the completion report with the pictures and the additional cost that was incurred.

Non-insurance claims are where we have the most issues. Some people would rather leave a rotting roof in place and hope the next storm wipes it out. I never want to leave something that's not safe. I am not someone who would rather save a dollar than do things the right way. Plus, there are huge liability issues when you don't do things the right way.

If a roofer finds something that needs to be done but wasn't included in the bid, he should always talk to the property owner before he does any work. Not communicating is bad for both parties in every single circumstance. You have to communicate to make things work. That's life in general. We don't want to be burdensome during the process, but at the same time, you've got to know what's going on. If a change is going to occur, the property owner should be the first person to know, not the last. The owner should have made that decision and been aware of it. In that circumstance, our company makes the owner aware of those things and then we follow up with the claims adjustor. We supplement the claim, and whenever you get that check, you just send it to us.

Why is it beneficial to let you talk to my insurance company and negotiate for me?

If you knew how to do this, you would be doing it already. If you knew all the ins and outs of the roofing and contracting business, we wouldn't be talking.

You need an expert to argue for you. You would never go to court without an attorney, but that's essentially what you are doing because the guy with the checkbook is going to come and tell you what he is going to do if you don't stop him. If you don't know any better, you are just going to let him do what he says. His mindset is, "I'm going to pay for what I say we're going to pay for and I'm not going to do it differently." Most insurance adjustors are called cat adjustors or catastrophe adjustors. They just look at the cosmetic exterior problems. They don't even look below the surface for anything that's not cosmetic. They want to fix what's going to make your property look pretty again and then you are going to go away. That's what they expect.

That person's job is to save money for the company, not to help you. My job is to get your property restored to the way it was before the loss, which is really what the adjustor's job is supposed to be. The adjustor's job is to return the property back to its position prior to loss. The underlying result is they are getting a salary and/or a commission from the insurance company to write claims based on their damage assessment.

You need a contractor on your side to fight for you. But the flip side of that is if you have taken the contractor's time to come and negotiate for you, you shouldn't beat him up on the price. That's one of the reasons contractors don't want to work with investors. They feel really underappreciated.

I know you are also an investor. What advice would you give to an investor who is going to hire a contractor?

Be straightforward from the get-go. Don't sugarcoat or hide anything. Use your gut instinct on people, but don't settle for less than what is required. You run a business. You have homeowner's insurance and you've got investment property umbrella coverage, and so forth, and you've got to prove that to people. Anybody who wants to work with you should demand the same. You should demand equal respect.

There are a lot of things you can do to choose a contractor. Look for somebody with a proven track record, somebody who is local and who has work they can show you. The best credentials are personal referrals or testimonials that let you know these people stand behind their work.

What do you think about the Better Business Bureau?

I think it is pointless. Most people don't even call and complain. If you have ever been to a McDonalds and not gotten your order right? Did you call and complain? You didn't because nothing was going to happen. You still didn't get the food you ordered.

You only have to be in business a couple of years before the BBB will let you pay to become a preferred member. They take your money and put you on their website, and if no one has called and complained about you, you have an A+ rating.

It's really a joke. The same way with a roofer's contracting license in the state of Oklahoma. It's less than $100. You fill out a piece of paper and submit your general liability insurance form to prove you have insurance. They don't even care what kind of insurance it is. The state is supposed to oversee this, but it's just another form of revenue.

You are a true insider. What tips can you give investors to help build their portfolios?

If you want the insider deal, leverage your insurance. Every time there is a storm, you should attempt to negotiate up to the next tier of shingles. If you went from three-tab, you go to architectural. If you go to architectural, you can negotiate architectural high-def. From high-def to class four would be a stretch because of the significant cost increase, but for the first couple of those, three-tab to twenty-year or twenty-five-year to a thirty-year, you should absolutely request an upgrade. If you have worked with that contractor before, they should grant that to you. If not, I wouldn't do business with them anymore.

Insurance claims factor in overhead and profit. Who gets that money?

The contractor. It's illegal for an insurer to put money in their pocket from the result of an insurance claim. The insurance claim is made to restore the property back to the position it was before the damage. If you had a TV that was destroyed by a storm and you didn't buy a TV, you didn't do what you should have done. You are supposed to replace the TV. It's the same thing with construction. But when real estate is damaged, the worst thing you can do is to not repair something because the insurance company wouldn't re-file the completion report if it's not line itemed on the report. They may even take the money back.

How can people get in touch with you when they need quality roof repair?

You can contact me on my mobile, 405-820-3878. I am the Vice President of Sales. We are a nationwide company. We do residential and commercial and have an entire metal division that does large commercial projects.

We do a lot of Mini Storage Units nationwide. We are respected by every major storage unit franchise. That would be one of our biggest acclaims in construction and in roofing.

Donny Ho

Tell us about your experience as an investor.

I don't have a background in investing, except for a few rental houses and some property management. I have been a general contractor on several jobs.

How long have you been around real estate investing?

Seven years.

How many times have you hired a contractor?

Hundreds. I have hired every contractor available, including plumbers, electricians, roofers, drywallers, and painters.

What's the worst experience you've had?

My worst experience didn't involve contractors. I made the mistake of renting out to almost anyone. I ran across a young couple that didn't fit my qualifications as renters. They were two young kids in their early twenties with a newborn. I felt sorry for them and agreed to let them live in my property despite the fact they didn't have first and last month's rent and didn't even have a bank account. Only the woman had a job. The man was unemployed.

It didn't take long before I had to chase them down for rent, and when they did pay, it was never the full amount. That got old pretty quickly, and it was soon time to kick them out. I followed the proper steps and filed the eviction.

After the tenants received the eviction letter, they said one of them stepped on a rusty nail and got infected. They also said the baby got sick from breathing in lead paint. When they left the home, they trashed everything in it. They broke the windows, pulled down the ceiling fan, and destroyed everything that could be destroyed.

Finding people to rent your investment is the easy part. Finding quality renters who will take care of your place is another.

And that lesson doesn't apply to just renters. It applies to contractors as well. If you don't take the time to bring in the right people from the start, you will live to regret it.

When you need to hire a contractor again, what will you do differently?

I would take more time to hire the right people. It takes a few tries to find the right members of your team. You have to know if the contractors you hire can deliver on their word and if they are reasonable in price. You might get lucky and find a good team off the bat, but that probably won't happen.

When you do find that team member who can deliver, start comparing prices. You pay for what you get, but when a contractor knows you own several houses, he thinks money grows on trees and looks for immediate opportunities rather than long-term business. Some people act stupid

Hiring Contractors

around large amounts of money, and everyone is always looking out for their own best interests. You can kill a sheep one time or you can shear a sheep forever. Some people get that and some people don't.

Master your industry and make a presence so that contractors know you. You will also learn who the bad apples are and avoid them.

What advice would you give to someone who needs to hire a contractor?

Know your stuff. Don't be afraid to ask questions and demand what you want. Contractors are a dime a dozen, and it's your job to weed out the professionals from the amateurs.

Never pay full price, and only pay half down for any large jobs you can't afford to be stiffed on. Never pay the full amount up front. Check references, and make sure contractors are licensed, insured, and bonded. Check for websites, online feedback, and anything else you can find on the Internet.

The most usefully tip is to ALWAYS have a signed contract and a copy of your contractor's address so you can sue him if things go wrong. Verbal agreements only work for $50 bucks or less. Be honest with yourself and your expectations and always hold the keys.

Price versus value. Any thoughts?

When I started, I wanted to pay as little as possible for everything and be the one making a profit while offering a competitive price. It can be achieved if you have the key players.

But price isn't everything. I would be happy to pay more if the job is done right the first time and it's done more quickly. Your time is worth money. It comes down to what your time is worth.

Bill Rosemeier, DinoSurfer Improvements

I have wanted to interview a contractor for a long time. I thought if we could hear a contractor speak about his experiences in dealing with investors, we could use that information to build our empires. I put an ad on Craigslist asking for input and expected to hear something right away. After six months, there was no response. I received a call from Bill Rosemeier out of the blue and he agreed to be interviewed. This information is a gold mine. It gives you and idea of how honest, decent contractors work and will help you keep them happy, as well as teach you how to weed out the bad contractors. Read this interview and use the information every time you hire someone to work with you. It will make your life easier and will help you keep great people.

Your perspective as a professional contractor is invaluable to my readers. Thank you for your time. What is the worst experience you've had when working as a contractor?

A lady contacted me to re-texture and repaint, and do some reconstruction to her entry, bathrooms, and kitchen. I gave her an appropriate timeline and a price for it, she agreed to it, and we signed a contract. My son and I did the first phase of the contract, which consisted of the entryway and two bathrooms. She was completely satisfied with that. It needed a little touch-up paint here and there, which is normal.

The next phase consisted of demolishing part of the wall the kitchen cabinets hung on. It was all demoed according to the specs and our agreement. There was lots of debris and dust. Plus, when you're demoing, tools get set down here and there. It looks pretty chaotic. The kitchen was pretty much demoed out, and everything was fine. She was completely happy with everything.

The ceiling was from the 1980s, and it had to go. We took that out, re-sheet-rocked it, re-textured it, and everything was great. It was looking really good. We applied the first coat of paint, installed recessed lighting, and everything was fine. She was happy with everything.

A few things came up (as they do in every remodel), and they got addressed. It was no big thing. When the third week started, she started doing things that were not acceptable. She started trying to dictate how I should do my job.

I've been doing this for over twenty years, and there is a process to doing a remodel. That's why I was hired to do it. I know what needs to be done, and I know how to do it. I bring decades of experience to the table. If I did things the way she wanted me to, I would have to redo my work several times.

The staining on the cabinets should be done at the end of the job to ensure that the lacquer and stain doesn't get on the walls. Woodwork is always done first, then the grid support. I wasn't doing things in the order she wanted, and it was really an issue for her. We got down to the last half of the day and she sent me an e-mail telling me to stop all the work.

I felt threatened. She put the job on hold while she left, and she also tried to dictate what days I had to show up. I'm a business. I just don't do one job at a time. I do four, five, six, or seven. I can't be at one job site all day long. It just doesn't work that way. I have my guys there. I don't know why she was so concerned about me being on site. We were three days ahead of schedule when all of this happened. I would have been finished with it at the end of the week.

She pulled the plug and I was out $4,000. My workmanship was flawless. All the materials were accounted for. Then to make it worse, her sons came into the picture. They were big and intimidated me and my help. I had serious concerns of being physically assaulted.

The next day I was supposed to install the cabinet doors and be done with that phase of the project. I ordered the doors and when I told her she needed to pay for them, which was in the agreement, and she said she don't order the doors. She had told me the day before to order the doors so she could see them installed.

As it stands now, I'm out $4,000 out of my pocket.

Why don't you just go to court and sue her?

I could go through all of that and draw this out into a long, long situation. I'm not interested in creating that kind of drama, even though it has been brought into in my life.

Hiring Contractors

I'm sure I could go to court and put a lien on that property. The judge would go for it and we'd have our day in court. Every year, I would have to go back and renew the lien. I think it's like $50 every year.

It might be ten or fifteen years down the road before she decides to sell the place, and I would only get my money if she actually sells it. If things work out like that, I could end up owning the house with all the interest tacked onto it.

Or I would die. She may plan on never moving so I may never see my money. I may get my money eventually, but what a headache. I've had to go through this before to get money. It causes a lot of stress.

My readers need contractors like you to work for us, and you need customers like my readers. What would you do differently and how can we both protect ourselves?

I would write the contract slightly differently, and I'm going to start doing this. When the job has multiple phases, the contract will state that no phase is set in stone. They may overlap each other, and adjustments may be made to each phase. There has to be a cutoff in the beginning for the next one, but not necessarily set in stone, and the contract will say that in the future. Customers should expect that flexibility is part of the process, and being flexible is the only way to have a successful relationship with a contractor.

For instance, when you're demoing a job and your demo is complete, you may have scratched some of the woodwork, and that's going to get refinished. You may have knocked a little hole in the sheet rock.

There's no use in putting stain and everything on the woodwork too early because you're going to be demoing tile, and tile is sharp. It's going to fly up and destroy the work that you've already done. Even if you cover everything with a heavy plastic tarp, tile will go right through that plastic. It's sharp. You have to use a face protector or you're going to get a bloody face from it. Demo hammers really knock that tile out. There's going to be lots and lots of dust, even though there's a dust barrier put up. Customers need to know things may need to be addressed and repaired at the end of the project. There is no way around it.

When you evaluate a job what goes through your mind? How do you charge?

A couple of different factors come into play. The duration of the job. How much the materials are going to cost. I try to add 10 to 20 percent to that for over-expenditures on material. In any reconstruction job or remodel, you are going to make mistakes, and I allow for those mistakes as best I can. If I go over the amount, it comes out of my side of it and I don't make any bones about it.

If I have a piece of four-by-eight finished cabinet grade plywood that cost $50 and I use it up and make mistakes on it, then I have to replace that out of my pocket. That's my fault. I make this clear to them and tell them, "I bought that."

If I underestimated the materials, there is a disclosure in my contract that states this is a general estimate for the materials. The cost listed may not represent the actual prices. There may be a 15 to 20 percent increase and those funds should be made available if needed.

How do you market your business? How can we find a good contractor?

I get most of my business through referrals. Those are set jobs I don't have to go out and bid against other people on. I'll average one or two of those a week. I've been doing this for over twenty years, and I have a pretty good following of people who seek me out. I have a waiting list. During the busy time of year it will sometimes grow to two to three months. When I slow down, I'm lucky to get three weeks to a month ahead.

I also charge a design and a consultation fee for my services. Those are nonrefundable. They're not part of the labor of the actual job. Some people can't understand that. I don't know why. I put that into my contract as well, explain it to them, and give them the reasons I charge those fees.

What do you think of Angie's List? Have you used it? Have you advertised on there?

About five or six years ago I used it a couple of times. We didn't get much feedback from customers.

How about Craigslist?

I use that daily. I get a lot of work from Craigslist. There's not a week that doesn't go by that I don't go out and do four to six estimates for people on bathrooms or kitchens. I specialize in bathrooms and kitchens. I can do a whole house, including add-ons, conversions, all kinds of stuff, but I focus on bathrooms and kitchens. That's my specialty.

How do you stay in contact with your customers?

I'm in constant daily contact with them, taking pictures, sending them pictures, asking them questions, asking them approval for a certain level reconstruct or something like that. I will send a text that reads, "Hey, you're okay with this part right here?" and send them a picture. That helps me get in and get out on an average remodel in about four days. I'm on my thirty-seventh one of the year so far, and it's only July.

Do your prices change when you're busy?

Yes, my rates go up during the busy time of the year. My normal rates for the summer are about 20 percent higher than in the wintertime when work slows down. I tell people if my rates are too high for you right now, wait until November or December, and I'll drop my rates 20 percent. Materials don't change, but the labor does.

Learn more about Bill and DinoSurfer at dinosurffer.com. He can be reached at 405-659-3808 and dinosurffer01@cox.net.

BONUS INTERVIEW

Jason Grotelueschen

Jason Grotelueschen is a relatively new Realtor. He has only been in the game since January 2013, but he is already killing it. Part of his success is due to a system called DISC, which helps define new prospects based on personality types. Once you understand a person's personality, you can interact with him the way that he understands the best. Use this technique when you meet with contractors. You will hire the right people the first time.

Tell us a little bit about yourself and why you got into real estate.

I was working eight to ten hours a day, five days a week, for the past sixteen years as a salesman. It would be equivalent to being a senior in high school for sixteen years. It was time to step out. It was time to make a change and move into the real world. Becoming a real estate investor was the best decision I ever made.

You deal with a lot of different people in real estate. I know that you use DISC to profile your prospects. How does that work?

My career and my understanding of people really didn't begin to unfold until after I left my eight-to-five job after sixteen years. When I got into real estate, I learned the DISC method, which is a system to understand basic personalities and how people act.

DISC is an acronym. "D" stands for dominance. It means how a person responds to problems and challenges. "I" stands for influence, and describes how a person influences others to his or her point of view. "S" is for steadiness, and reflects how a person responds to the pace of the environment. "C" is compliance for how a person responds to rules and procedures that are set by others.

We all have a makeup of "D", "I", "S", and "C". I'm 88 percent "S", 88 percent "C", 50 percent "D", and about 12 percent "I". In a given situation, the personality trait that comes out in me is predominantly steadiness and compliance.

What was the light bulb moment when you realized DISC was important?

I joined a great training program where they trained real estate agents in DISC and taught them to understand personalities. When I meet a prospect, I ask myself, "What is his personality? Which part of the DISC is he using to understand a situation?" I am trained to look for that so that I can develop rapport.

Let's run through a scenario. You're trying to sell a property. It's an average home, a three-bedroom, two-bath, two-car garage house with a price of $150,000. What would your presentation be to a "D", and then "I", and then an "S", and then to a "C"?

"Ds" will walk through the rooms quickly. They're out to kill something,

Hiring Contractors

and I don't waste time. I get straight to the point and ask them if they want to buy the house. "Do you want to buy the house? I can get you the house." I go straight to the point. That speaks to their "D". They want to kill it and drag it home.

For an "I", everything's a party. I bring out the energy, touch their elbows and use arm gestures. They want to feel everything's happy. They use a lot of body language when they're talking and they want to feel, "We want to bring people over after we move in." I tell them if we can get you in this house, you can have people over. Invite your friends. They get their energy being around other people, so I try to paint a mental picture for them with other people in the house. They're connectors, and they appreciate that.

With an "S", I slow my speech down and I make eye contact. I use a lot of feeling words. I say, "So, how do you feel about this house? How did you feel when you walked up? How does it make you feel to think about buying this house? How will you feel after you close and you walk in and you set your keys on the counter?" It's mainly about feeling. I put my hand on their shoulder, look them in the eye, and walk them through the house, that kind of thing. I slow down and speak to their feelings.

"Cs" walk in and they're looking for details. They go and look at the water heater, they look at the furnace, they'll climb up in the attic, and they'll want manuals. I know the details when I go into the house. I'm ready for that. I know how old the roof is and what kind of shingles it has. I state the obvious. Then I go into further detail, "Here's what your monthly payment will be. Are you paying cash? Here's what your net on investment would be if you pay cash. Here's what your return on your investment would be. Here's what your cash flow might be." "Cs" are analytical.

Have you found a specific personality profile that you like to work with, or is there a personality you want to avoid?

The main benefits of understanding DISC are building rapport and getting referrals. If I understand personality types, I'm less likely to irritate people. I can build rapport and people will want to give me referrals. That's first and foremost.

Who do I want in my database? They all have their strengths. They all have their weaknesses. But I probably want "Ds". They're just out to kill it. "Is" are networkers. "S" personalities will chew off an arm to help me. They'll go to great lengths to support me. I will call "Cs" when I need details, when I need people that can be there as support to inspectors.

Do you use DISC when you hire contractors or buy real estate?

Definitely. "Cs" make great inspectors. They are super-detailed and will go through every inch of the house. They come into their own and really shine when they have a little bit of "I" and maybe some "S." Those personality types not only address concerns about the house, but they'll also address my clients. They are a calming force. They will tell them things like, "Here's what we found. It's not bad. It's not good. It's just what we found." They're just facts and they'll be able to address the needs of my buyer.

If I'm marketing a property, I'm contacting every "I" on my list. They are networkers, the people who know people. I love to work with "Is" when it comes to getting the word out. You can't do any better.

I will call an "S" when I need support. They are great to talk with or bounce an idea off of. An "S" with a combination of "C" is really good asset.

"D" personalities are their own animals. They're there when you need somebody to talk about a business idea. Entrepreneurs are usually high "Ds" and "Is". They give me great feedback and help me make sure I'm doing the right things.

Tell us about a time you read someone's personality profile and were able to use that to your advantage.

Here's one that started as a failure but turned into a win. I had some clients I misread. I thought they were very low "Is". As I got to know them better, I knew the wife was an off-the-charts "S". Everything was filtered through her emotions. I thought she was a "C". She's quiet. I just misread it. The husband was a mild "I". He didn't have a lot of energy and may have been an "I"/"S". He was very stable and had the same job for years and years,

Because I misread them, I wasn't giving them the attention they craved. They wanted to feel they had my full attention, but I was playing it a little more hands off and was just feeding them facts.

We put in an offer and it fell through. The husband called and said they wanted their earnest money back. Then the wife called and laid into me. She was not happy at all. I met with the husband, and we sat down and talked. Because I had misread them, I wasn't giving them the attention they wanted. The worst thing for an "I" is to show them that somebody doesn't like them, because they think life's a party. They want to connect with everybody and bring everybody together. He thought I was upset with him, which wasn't true. I always try to leave my feelings out of the situation when it comes to fulfilling the needs of my clients.

I apologized. "It's my fault. I misread you guys. I misjudged it. You guys just aren't feeling it, are you?"

"No, we're not feeling it."

That's when I knew I had an "S" and "I"/"S" on my hands. I turned it around and focused solely on addressing their feelings. I started using feeling words and called them on the phone asking how they were doing and how they felt about the houses I showed them. Now they are avid clients. They told me, "You are our realtor. We're not using anybody else. We're going to use you for everything." They were ready to turn me into the real estate police before I read them properly and changed how I communicated with them. Once I started to address their personalities and used their language, they turned right around. They're fans for life.

What advice would you give investors to help build their businesses using DISC?

The first thing an investor should do is to take a personality profile. There are a bunch of them. There's a prominent DISC website where you can take the profile test for free. Once you understand who you are, you can understand the different personality types. There's more than one way to look at life. You understand people have differing personalities and different ways of looking at things.

I met an individual who was in a really bad situation with drugs and divorce. I was able to focus on his needs and his personality, which will probably mean I will get the contract to sell his house. That wouldn't have happened if I didn't identify his personality and connect with him.

As a real estate investor, it's important to know who you are and where you fall on the DISC. You will know if you're dominant, the influencer, steady, or precise. Once you know your strengths, you can improve or eliminate your weaknesses. Practice all the personality types and learn how to turn them on and off. And practice identifying hem in other people.

You'll run across people who are in different situations, and you need to know how to handle them. You may meet a dominant who has to get rid of a house and he wants to make it happen now. He doesn't have time to waste. The best thing you can say is, "Hey, I don't want to waste your time here. Do you want to sell your house? I have a buyer." That's what you can do with a "D".

"Is" are the life of the party and they want you to like them, so you treat them like friends. You can't hold back on that. You can control the situation and connect with them.

The "S" is steady. They need someone to focus on their feelings and how they're doing. If you're a "D", you may not want to take the time to do that, but it's time to switch that off and turn into an "S".

"Cs" want to get the details. Let's look ahead and say it'll be okay.

It's about developing rapport. We all use scripts every day in our lives. Practice those scripts with different personality traits. It's a matter of knowing what to say in the right situation to help people. That's what it's all about.

TEN EMPOWERING TIPS

Before you sign a check and hand over your hard-earned money, read the following tips. Apply them before any contractor sets foot on your property. Every contractor depends on referrals. That gives you, the customer and potential source of business, a lot of power. Use it to your advantage.

Empowering Tip 1: Research, Research, Research, and Then Do Some More Research. It is your responsibility to know as much about what goes into every job as you can. Always ask about:

- Material costs (check online for prices);
- Whether the estimate is fixed, or if there could be fluctuations based on something out of the contractor's control;
- When he is going to start, how long is it going to take, and when will the job be finished; and
- Factors that could delay the completion time.

Empowering Tip 2: Have a Plan Before You Start. Never start a project without having a clear plan. Having a detailed outline of the work that is going to be performed will ensure you and your contractor are on the same page. You don't want to get halfway through and realize that what the contractor has done is nothing like what you imagined. That's going to delay the project and cost you money.

Empowering Tip 3: Things Are Going to Get Messy. Ripping out a ceiling, demolishing a wall, or removing tile from a bathroom will create more dust than you can imagine. Don't let this shock you. A competent contractor would have let you know this was going to happen in advance and would have covered up floors and furniture with plastic before he started working. Don't be shocked at how messy a job site will become.

Empowering Tip 4: Let the Contractor Do His Job. You have the right to show up at a job site everyday to inspect the work and ask a few questions. But the contractor and his workers don't want to hold a long conversation with you about the cost of gasoline or how hard it is for you to find a babysitter. Good contractors want to work and get the job done, so stay out of their way and let them perform their tasks. Keep it professional.

Empowering Tip 5: Most Jobs Do Not Run as Smoothly as You or the Contractor Would Like. Many things can slow down a construction project:
- Weather;
- Materials or parts not delivered on time;
- Crew members who quit or are fired;

- The contractor's previous job not finishing on time;
- Unexpected discoveries, such as termites, electrical problems, or plumbing issues; or
- Subcontractors not finishing on time.

If these things happen, don't get angry. Take a breath, don't take it personally, and make sure your contractor understands the importance of getting your project done as quickly as possible.

Empowering Tip 6: Steps to Lowering Your Cost or Speeding Up the Job. If you want to save money, use day labor from Craigslist or Labor Ready, but be sure to ask the contractor if this will help. If they are smart, and most contractors are, they will give you all the dirty, time consuming, and crummy jobs they do not like doing, such as:

- Ripping out the floor, ceiling, or tile and taking everything to the dump;
- Picking up materials and supplies;
- The final cleanup; and
- Hiring individual sub-contractors to do each separate job.

Empowering Tip 7: Establish a Budget and Stick to Your Guns. Know what you are going to spend before the project starts. Don't show up with a blank check and hope for the best.

Always get an estimate in writing, and make sure the contractor sticks to it. On some projects, a contractor should be able to give you an exact estimate. On a painting job, the contractor can easily look at and understand all the work and materials that are needed for the project. He should give an exact quote.

However, if you are installing a new kitchen, the contractor cannot be sure what he is going to find after the backsplash is removed. He could discover exposed electrical wires that are about to short out and cause a fire. An electrician would have to repair the wires before any work could be done. Termite damage may cause further delays and expenses as well. Those are expenses the contractor could not have foreseen, and your budget should take that into account.

Empowering Tip 8: Most Contactors Want to Do a Good Job. Use That to Your Advantage. Despite what you might have heard or read, most contractors want you to be happy with their work. They want you to give them a positive reference once the job is done. If you respect them, they usually give you their best effort.

Empowering Tip 9: Ask Around. You have the most power before the project starts. Don't sign on the dotted line until you have the right guy

Ask your friends, family, neighbors, and co-workers for recommendations. They have already screened potential contractors. Don't reinvent the wheel. Use that information.

If you are hiring a painting contractor, head over to the local paint store and ask them what painting companies buy the most paint. The contractors buying all the paint are also getting all the jobs. There is usually a reason for that.

Hiring Contractors

Drive around neighborhoods and look for construction signs in the yard or on work trucks. When you find one, stop in, have a look around, and start up a conversation with the contractor. Get to know contractors as they are working, and you can see how they take care of things. You can also get a sneak peek of their work.

Empowering Tip 10: Negotiate a Payment Schedule That Protects You. Never pay a contractor in full before the job is done. Once you pay, you don't have any leverage. Savvy investors make sure the final check is not written until the work is complete and they are satisfied with the results.

TIME TO ROLL

"Time is more valuable than money. You can get more money, but you cannot get more time."

-Jim Rohn

You have reached the end of this book, but this is the beginning of a new chapter in your investing career. You now have the information you need to make better decisions when you hire a contractor.

But none of this knowledge will do you any good if you don't take action. It's one thing to read this book. It's another to consistently apply the knowledge I have shared with you. Some people will learn something new, think about all the ways they can use it, have a few big dreams, and then do absolutely nothing. Their goals will fly by as life leaves them in the dust.

Don't be one of those people. Do the things that others aren't willing to do. It's the only way to build your empire and live the life you have earned.

Do your due diligence, hire the right people, and don't be afraid to pull the trigger. And may your next deal be your best deal.

I want to hear about your successes and learn from your failures. Drop me a line at (405) 633-1008 to tell me how your empire is growing. You can also e-mail me at info@thesavvylandlordbook.com.

LEARN CONTRACTOR LINGO: TERMINOLOGY

"The road to success is always under construction."

-Lily Tomlin

When you talk to contractors, sometimes you will think they are speaking a foreign language. They will use terms you have never heard, and you won't understand half of what they say. You have to get on the same page, or you will waste your two most valuable assets: time and money.

Below you will find a list of contractor terminology that will help you understand what your contractor is saying. Learn these words and you will feel empowered. When you learn these definitions, you can take control of conversations. I would recommend scanning a category right before you meet with a contractor so that the terms are fresh on your mind.

ROOFING

Architectural (Laminate): a shingle normally heavier in weight that has more definition or depth than the shingle itself. Strip shingles made of two separate pieces laminated together to create extra thickness.

Deck: a top surface to which a roof system is applied; a surface installed over the supporting framing members.

Learn Contractor Lingo: Terminology

Downspout: a pipe for draining water from roof gutters to a drain; also called a leader.

Drip Edge: an L-shaped flashing used along eaves and rakes to allow water run-off into the gutters and to drip clear of underlying construction.

Eave: a part of the roof that overhangs or extends outward and is not directly over the exterior walls or the building's interior.

Felt: a fibrous material used as an underlayment or sheathing paper; roll roofing materials.

Flashing: sheet metal on structures that projects vertically from the roof to create a watertight seal between the roof and the structure.

Gable: the end of an exterior wall that meets in a triangular point at the ridge of a sloping roof.

Pitch: the rise of a rafter as it projects along a horizontal plane. If a roof has a six and twelve pitch, it would mean that a roof rises six inches for every twelve inches of horizontal run.

Rafter: a supporting framing that makes up the roof structure; immediately beneath the deck; the roof sheathing is nailed to the rafters.

Self Sealing: a shingle with an asphalt strip underneath it after it is applied and subjected to heat it seals to the shingle underneath it.

Starter Shingle: the first row of shingles that are installed at the bottom of the roof. These overlap the eave metal and are normally turned upside-down and backwards to produce a straight line along the leading edge of the eave metal.

Steep Slope: roof pitches that are more than forty-five degrees.

Square: the area of coverage of a shingle. One square is equal to 100 square feet.

Three Tab: a shingle that is broken into three tabs.

Toe Board: a two-by-four or a wood member that is nailed to the roof in order to allow roofers to stand and work without slipping off the roof.

Truss: a combination of beams, bars and ties, usually in triangular units, that form a framework for support.

Water Bond: the slots in shingles that provide a path for water to drain off a roof. The water bonds normally line up in the application of roof shingles and create an avenue for water to drain.

Valley: an internal angle formed by the intersection of two inclined roof surfaces that provide water runoff.

HVAC (HEATING, VENTILATION, & AIR CONDITIONING)

A-Coil: a heating or cooling element made of pipe or tubing, usually with plates or fins.

Air Conditioning: a process of controlling the temperature, humidity, cleanliness, and distribution of air.

British Thermal Unit (BTU): the amount of heat necessary to change the temperature of one pound of pure water one degree Fahrenheit.

Check Valve: a valve designed to permit flow in one direction only.

Compression: a reduction of volume of a vapor or gas by mechanical means.

Learn Contractor Lingo: Terminology

Compression Ratio: a ratio determined by dividing the discharge pressure, in PSI, by the suction pressure in PSI.

Compressor: a mechanical device used to compress gases. There are three main types: reciprocating, centrifugal, and rotary.

Condensing Unit: a term used for the portion of a refrigeration system where the compression and condensation of refrigerant is accomplished. Also referred to as the high side.

Cycle: a complete course of operation of a refrigerant back to a selected starting point in a system.

Discharge Line: a tube used to convey the compressed refrigerant vapor from the compressor to the condenser inlet.

Discharge Pressure: a pressure read at the compressor outlet. Also called head pressure or high side pressure.

Evaporator: a device in which a liquid refrigerant is vaporized.

Filter-Drier: a device that removes moisture, acid, and foreign matter from the refrigerant.

Heat Exchanger: a type of device used for the transfer of heat energy from the source to the conveying medium.

Integrated Hot Water System: a system that provides water heating from a single heat source.

Pressure Drop: a decrease in pressure due to friction of a fluid or vapor as it passes through a tube, duct, or lift.

Pump Down: the process of pumping refrigerant out of the evaporator and suction line at the end of the on-cycle by closing a solenoid valve in the liquid line and letting the compressor shut-off.

Refrigerant Distributor: a type of device that meters equal quantities of refrigerant to independent circuits in the evaporator coil.

Relay: a device used to open and close an electrical circuit. A relay may be actuated by a bimetal electrically heated strip, a rod wrapped with a fine resistance wire causing expansion when energized, a bellows actuated by expansion of a fluid, gas, or an electromagnetic coil.

Reversing Valve: a device in a heat pump that is electrically controlled to reverse the flow of refrigerant as the system is switched from cooling to heating. Also called a four-way valve.

Riser: A vertical tube or pipe that carries refrigerant in any form from a lower to a higher level.

Saturation: a condition of stable equilibrium of a vapor and a liquid.

Split System: an air conditioner or heat pump that has components in two different locations (typically one inside and one outside).

Static Pressure: a type of normal force per unit area at a small hole in the wall of a duct.

Suction Line: a tube used to convey the refrigerant vapor from the evaporator outlet to the suction inlet of compressor.

Thermostat: a bimetal actuated switch to close and open a circuit to indicate or terminate operation of a heating or air conditioning system.

Thermostatic Expansion Valve: a refrigerant control that monitors the flow rate according to the superheat at the evaporator outlet.

Vacuum: any pressure below atmospheric pressure.

Vapor Barrier: an impervious layer of material superimposed upon a layer of insulation. Vapor barriers are always applied on the warm side of the insulation layer.

ELECTRICAL

Alternating Current (AC): an electric current that changes direction with a regular frequency.

American Wire Gauge (AWG): a standard measure that represents the size of wire. The larger the number the thinner the wire.

Breaker Panel: an electrical service panel that contains house breakers. Most homes have an electrical panel outside which holds the main breakers and all of the 220-volt breakers. There will also be another panel inside the house that will contain all the 110-volt breakers.

Brownout: a reduction in voltage and/or power when demand for electricity exceeds generating capacity. The term brownout is misleading because customers generally do not notice the reduction, except when it affects sensitive electronic equipment.

Capacitor: a device that stores an electrical charge, usually by means of conducting plates or foil separated by a thin insulating layer of dielectric material. The effectiveness of the device, or its capacitance, is measured in Farads.

Circuit Breaker: a device designed to open and close a circuit by non-automatic means and to open the circuit automatically on a pre-determined over current without damage to itself when properly applied within its rating.

Conductor Bare: a conductor having no covering or electrical insulation whatsoever.

Connector: a Romex connector or an EMT conduit connector. A Romex connector is used to connect Romex cable to electrical boxes. EMT connectors are used to connect EMT conduit to electrical boxes.

Covered: a conductor encased within material of composition and thickness that is not recognized as electrical insulation.

Current: a flow of electricity commonly measured in amperes.

Diode: an electronic semiconductor device that predominantly allows current to flow in only one direction.

Direct Current (DC): a circuit in which the flow of electrons is in one direction only, from anode to cathode.

Electronic Ballasts: an electronic device that regulates the voltage of fluorescent lamps. Compared to older magnetic ballasts, electronic ballasts use less electricity and are not prone to the flickering and humming effects sometimes associated with magnetic ballasts.

EMT: a thin-walled metal electrical conduit. Before flexible PVC conduit was accepted for commercial use, EMT was the main conduit product used in commercial construction. EMT conduit did not need to be threaded

Learn Contractor Lingo: Terminology

and was bent to meet the requirements of the job. EMT has fittings such as connectors and couplings in order to connect the individual pieces and connect to metal boxes.

Fault: a short circuit in an electrical system.

Fuse: a protective electrical device. A fuse is rated for a maximum amount of current flow, which is measured in amps. When the current flow exceeds the amperage rating on the fuse, the fuse link in the fuse will open and stop the flow of current. Most fuses have been replaced with electrical breakers.

Ground Rod: a copper or aluminum rod half an inch in diameter and eight feet long. It is driven in the ground near the outside electrical service and is used as an electrical ground for the house electrical service.

Ground (Wire): a conducting connection, whether intentional or accidental, between an electrical circuit or equipment and the earth, or to some conducting body that serves in place of the earth.

Home Run: the main line that runs from the electrical service panel to the first device in the electrical circuit.

Insulator: any material that does not allow electrons to flow through it.

Insulated: a conductor encased within material of composition and thickness that is recognized as electrical insulation.

Interrupter: an element designed to interrupt specific currents under specified conditions.

Keyless: a single-bulb electrical device used normally in a storage area or for temporary lighting. The fixture is a white porcelain fixture.

Kilowatt (kW): real power delivered to a load (W x 1,000 VA).

Kilowatt-hour: a unit of energy or work equal to one kilowatt for one hour, abbreviated as kWh or KWH. The normal quantity used for metering and billing customers for electricity.

Limit Switch: a switch operated by some part or motion of a power-driven machine or equipment to alter the electric circuit associated with the machine or equipment.

Low Voltage: power to some electronic devices operating on a voltage level much lower than the standard 110 volts, such as doorbells and thermostats.

Meter Base: a mounting plate for a watt-hour meter.

Ohm: a unit of measure for resistance.

Outlet: a point on the wiring system at which current is taken to supply utilization equipment.

Overload: an operation of equipment in excess of normal, full-load rating, or of a conductor in excess of rated ampacity that, when it persists for a sufficient length of time, would cause damage or dangerous overheating. A fault, such as a short circuit or ground fault, is not an overload.

Overvoltage: a voltage above the normal rated voltage or the maximum operating voltage of a device or circuit. A direct test overvoltage is a voltage above the peak of the line alternating voltage.

Pigtail: a temporary electrical light device consisting of a light socket and two connecting wires.

Phase: a classification of an AC circuit. They are usually single-phase

Learn Contractor Lingo: Terminology

(two wires or three wire), two-phase (three wires or four wires), or three-phase (three wire or four wire).

Receptacle: an electrical device used to furnish an electrical source for electrical tools or appliances. Receptacles can provide either 110-volts or 220-volts.

Resistor: material that limits the flow of current when voltage is applied.

Romex: electrical wiring consisting of wires wrapped in a plastic sheath. It is generally used in newer homes.

Switch: an electrical device used to turn other devices on and off by opening or closing the electrical connection to the device.

Switch Leg: the wire connected to the switch, which controls the on and off of the device.

Temporary pole: an electrical pole that provides electrical power during a construction project. The pole consists of a breaker box and receptacles to allow construction tools to be plugged in.

Transformer: a static electrical device that uses electromagnetic induction and transfers electrical energy from one circuit to another, usually with changed values of voltage and current in the process.

Transient: a type of high amplitude, short duration pulse superimposed on the normal voltage.

Two Gang: an electrical box that holds two switches, two receptacles, or one switch and one receptacle.

Volt: an electrical potential difference or pressure across a one ohm resistance carrying a current of one ampere. Named after Italian physicist Count Alessandro Volta (1745-1827).

Wire Nut: a device used to connect multiple wires together. They provide a good electrical connection after twisting the wire nut tightly.

Watt: a unit of power equal to the rate of work represented by a current of one ampere under a pressure of one volt.

PLUMBING

ABS (Aristocraft bristone styrine): a rigid black plastic piping used for waste, vent, and drain lines.

Access Panel: an opening in the wall or ceiling near the fixture that allows access for servicing the plumbing or electrical system.

Air Gap: the vertical distance between the water supply outlet and the flood level rim of the fixture it discharges into, such as the distance between the faucet and the top of the sink.

Angle Stop (Cut Off): a shut-off valve between the water pipes and a faucet. Its inlet connects to the water supply pipe in a wall, and its outlet angles up ninety degrees toward the faucet. These are used to shut off water to a fixture in case of an emergency.

Basket Strainer: a basket-shaped strainer with holes and a slot that fits into a sink or shower drain. They allow water to run out but catch food or other objects before they can enter the sewage system and possibly clog the drain.

Learn Contractor Lingo: Terminology

Bleed: draining a pipe, tube, or hose of excess air by opening a valve at the end or systematically removing the air by force or suction.

Check Valve: a type of backflow preventer installed in a pipe run that allows water to flow in only one direction.

Clean Out: an access point to the sanitary or waste lines, which allows them to be cleaned if they are clogged.

Closet Auger: a flexible rod with a curved end used to access a toilet's built-in trap and remove clogs.

Compression Fitting: tubing or pipe connection where a nut and a sleeve or ferrule are placed over a copper or plastic tube and are compressed tightly around the tube. As the nut is tightened, a positive grip and seal are formed without soldering.

Compression Valve: a valve used for water faucets. It is opened or closed by raising or lowering a horizontal disk on a threaded stem.

Copper Type: the copper normally used in pressure or water applications in residential construction. Type K or type L is preferable. The higher in letter the thinner the copper will be.

Coupling: a vent pipe hood, which protects it from the elements.

CPVC (Chlorinated Polyvinyl Chloride): a rigid plastic pipe used in water supply systems.

Dry Fit: coupling sections of pipe together without any glue or solder to ensure a proper fit.

Elbow: a fitting that forms a ninety-degree angle.

Female Fitting: a fitting that receives a pipe or fitting into which another fitting is inserted.

Fixture: devices that provide a supply of water or its disposal, such as sinks, tubs, and toilets.

Flapper Valve: a part on the bottom of the toilet tank that opens to allow water to flow from the tank into the bowl.

Float Ball: a floating ball connected to the ballcock inside the toilet tank that rises or falls with water.

Floor Flange or /Flange: a fitting that connects a toilet to a floor drain.

Flushometer: a toilet valve that automatically shuts off after it meters a certain amount of water flow.

Flux: a type of paste applied to copper pipes and fittings before soldering to help the fusion process and prevent oxidation.

Gray Water: waste water from sinks, showers, and bathtubs but not toilets.

Joints: plumbing connections in copper or plastic.

Lateral: branching off supply lines for water or sewer.

Manifold: a fitting that connects a number of branches to the main; serves as a distribution point.

O.D.: outside diameter.

O-Ring: a round rubber washer used to create a watertight seal, chiefly around valve stems.

Pee Trap: the sanitary trap normally at the beginning of a drain underneath lavatories or sinks.

Learn Contractor Lingo: Terminology

Perk Test: a test to determine how well soil allows water to penetrate, percolate, or perk. This test determines if a septic tank can be used in a particular location on a piece of property.

Pipe Dope: slang for pipe-joint compound. Substance applied to thread fittings to create a watertight seal.

Plumb: precisely vertical, or to test for or to make vertical; to perform plumbing work.

Plumber's Putty Pliable: popular putty used to seal joints between drain pieces and fixture surfaces.

Plunger: an instrument with a rubber head used to create suction in a drain line or a toilet to push a clog through the line.

Pop-Up Drain: a type of drain assembly for lavatory and bath. When a lavatory lift rod or bath overflow plate lever is lifted, the pop-up drain closes so the lavatory or tub retains water.

Pressure Balance Valve: a shower mixing valve that automatically maintains balance between incoming hot and cold water supplies by regulating fluctuations in pressure. As a result, temperature remains constant. Also known as an anti-scald valve.

Pressure Tank: a device used to pump water from a well.

Pressure Test: pressurizing a plumbing line to see if it maintains a constant pressure.

PVC (Polyvinyl Chloride): a rigid white or cream-colored plastic pipe used in non-pressure systems, such as drainage, waste, and vent systems.

Hiring Contractors

Reducer: a fitting that connects pipes of different sizes.

Riser: a vertical metal or plastic tube or assembly that connects a faucet to the water supply stop valve, usually made of copper.

Rough-In: installation of the drain, waste, vent, and supply lines in a structure to the proposed location of each fixture.

Rough Plumbing: a stage in construction when the plumbing is actually roughed in before the walls are covered.

Run: a complete or secondary section of pipe that extends from the supply to fixture or drain to stack.

Saddle Valve: a valve mounted on a pipe run by a clamping device or fitting that taps into the side of a pipe. Used to make a quick connection to an existing line in order to provide a water supply.

Sleeve: a pipe that is passed through a wall for the purpose of inserting another pipe through it.

Slip Joint: a connection made with compression fittings.

Solder: a metal alloy melted to create a fused joint between metal pieces. The act of melting solder into the joint.

Stack Test: filling a stand pipe normally ten feet in height with water and letting it sit for a period of time. This normally tests the sanitary drain in a house or inner foundation.

Stand Pipe: open vertical pipe that receives water from a washing machine. A high vertical pipe or reservoir that is used to secure a uniform pressure in a water-supply system.

Learn Contractor Lingo: Terminology

Stop Valve: a shut-off valve under sinks and toilets that allows the water supply to be cut off to one fixture without affecting the water supply to other fixtures.

Trap: a curved section of drain line that prevents sewer odors from escaping into the atmosphere. All fixtures with drains must have "P" traps installed. A toilet is the only plumbing fixture with an "S" trap.

Union: a three-piece fitting that joins two sections of pipe, but allows them to be disconnected without cutting the pipe.

Valve Seat: a non-moving part of a valve. Water flow is stopped when the moveable portion of the valve comes in contact with the valve seat.

Vent: a pipe that allows air into a drain system to balance the air pressure, preventing water in the traps from being siphoned off.

Waste & Overflow: a drain assembly for a bathtub. The outlet at the top removes the overflow water during tub filling and the drain at the bottom removes wastewater when the tub is drained.

CONCRETE

Aggregate: a mixture of sand, rock, crushed stone, expanded materials, or particles that typically compose 75 percent of concrete by volume. It improves the formation and flow of cement paste and improve the concrete's structural performance.

Broom Finish: concrete that has been brushed with a broom when fresh in order to improve its traction or to create a distinctive fine-lined texture.

Cement Types:

Type I: general purpose cement suitable for practically all uses in residential construction but should not be used where it will be in contact with high sulfate soils or be subject to excessive temperatures during curing.

Type II: used where precaution against moderate sulfate attack is important, as in drainage structures where sulfate concentrations in groundwater are higher than normal.

Type III: used when high strengths are desired at very early periods, usually a week or less. It is used when there is a desire to remove forms as soon as possible or to put the concrete into service quickly.

Type IV: special cement used where the amount and rate of heat generated during curing must be kept to a minimum. The development of strength is slow and is intended in large masses of concrete such as dams.

Type V: special cement intended for use only in construction exposed to severe sulfate action, such as western states where soil has high alkali content.

Concrete: a hardened building material created by combining a mineral (which is usually sand, gravel, or crushed stone), a binding agent (natural or synthetic cement), chemical additives, and water.

Concrete Mixture: a percentage of cement content contained in the concrete. A rich mixture contains a high proportion of cement. A lean mixture is a mixture of concrete or mortar with relatively low cement content. A harsh mixture of concrete is one without mortar or aggregate fines, resulting in an undesirable consistency and workability.

Curing: a process of maintaining freshly placed concrete, mortar, plaster, or grout at a particular temperature for a period of time so that the desired properties of the mix can develop properly.

Dowel: a cylindrical piece of stock inserted into holes in adjacent pieces of material to align and/or attach the two pieces.

Float: a tool (not a darby) usually made of wood, aluminum, magnesium, rubber, or sponge. Used in concrete or tile finishing operations to impart a relatively even but still open texture to an unformed fresh concrete surface.

Floating: bringing water to the surface of concrete by using a hand float or bull float. The operation of finishing a fresh concrete or mortar surface by use of a float.

Form: a temporary erected structure or mold used for the support and containment of concrete during placement and while it is setting and gaining sufficient strength to be self-supporting.

Form Board: a board used to form up or build the form of concrete until it has set.

Hand float: a wooden tool used to lay on and to smooth or texture a finish coat of plaster or concrete.

Jitterbug: a tool used when pouring concrete.

Joint: a position where two or more building materials, components, or assemblies are put together, fixed or united, with or without the use of extra jointing products.

Mason: one who builds with brick, stones, masonry, or concrete.

Masonry: construction composed of shaped or molded units, usually small enough to be handled by one man and composed of stone, ceramic brick, tile, concrete, glass, or adobe.

Mortar: a mixture of cement (or lime) with sand and water used in masonry work.

Mud: slang for cement or mortar.

Pea Gravel: concrete aggregate passing the 1/2" sieve and retained on a No. 4 sieve.

Plain Concrete: concrete either without reinforcement or reinforced only for shrinkage or temperature changes.

Ready-Mixed Concrete: concrete batched or mixed at a central plant before it is delivered to a construction site andi ready for placement. It is also known as transit-mixed concrete.

Rebar: reinforcing bar-ribbed steel bars installed in foundation concrete walls, and footers and poured in place in concrete structures designed to strengthen concrete. Rebar comes in various thicknesses and strength grades.

Reinforced Concrete: concrete reinforced by the addition of steel bars, making it more able to tolerate tension and stress.

Slump: the consistency of concrete mix. A slump test will determine the consistency between batches and the concrete's workability, and

Learn Contractor Lingo: Terminology

is especially important in foundation work. Slump is tested by pouring concrete in a metal container and letting it sit for a period of time, then assessing the distance in which it drops. The greater the distance, the higher (wetter) the slump.

Steel trowel: a smooth concrete finish obtained with a steel trowel. Also a tool used for non-porous smooth finishes of concrete. A flat steel tool used to spread and smooth plaster, mortar, or concrete. Pointing trowels are small enough to be used in places where larger trowels will not fit. The pointing trowel has a point. The common trowel has a rectangular blade attached to a handle. For a smooth finish, the steel trowel is used when the concrete begins to stiffen.

Steel Troweling: a type of steel hand tool or machine used to create a dense, smooth finish on a concrete surface.

Straightedge: a rigid and straight piece of wood or metal used to strike off or screed a concrete surface to the proper grade, or to check the flatness of a finished grade.

Strike Off: to remove concrete in excess of that which is required to fill the form evenly or bring the surface to grade. This is performed with a straight-edged piece of wood or metal.

Yard of concrete: one cubic yard of concrete is 3 feet x 3 feet x 3 feet in volume, or 27 cubic feet. One cubic yard of concrete will pour 80 square feet of 3.5' sidewalk or basement/garage floor.

Bed Joint: a horizontal mortar bed that the bricks are laid upon. The mortar is spread on top of the course below and the bricks are laid to the string line on top of the mortar.

Brick Ledge: a depression placed in the outside perimeter of the house wherever brick will be located. This is 5-1/2" wide and 1-1/2" deep.

Brick Trowel: a type of tool used to spread mortar and lay brick. It is also used to make brick cuts and remove excess mortar from the brick course as the brick are being laid.

Course: one layer or row of bricks.

Head Joint: a vertical mortar joint where two bricks butt together at the end of a brick. When laying brick, these joints should be straight vertically. With king- or queen-size bricks, these bricks will stagger but will be straight vertically respectively.

Mortar: a mixture of sand, a binder such as lime, and water. On construction sites, the mortar mix comes in bags and the mason sand and water are mixed together on the job site.

Rake Joint: the type of mortar joint that will be in the brick. After the mortar dries, a joiner is used to rake out a groove about one-quarter of an inch thick.

Running Bond: courses of brick that are laid with staggering head joints. This is the most common bond when laying brick. If a running bond is being used with modular brick, the end of the brick will be at the midpoint of the brick on the course below.

Wall Ties: corrugated galvanized metal strips used in residential construction. Wall ties are bent to form a ninety-degree angle and are nailed to the wall usually every six courses vertically and every stud horizontally.

FOUNDATION

Anchor Bolt: a large metal bolt embedded in the outside perimeter of most concrete foundations. These bolts come in different diameters. The most common one used in residential building is one-half by six inches. Sometimes referred to as "J" bolts because of their shape. These bolts are used to anchor bottom plates to the foundation.

Back Fill: back filling against a form, retaining wall, or bulkhead to provide support for the form or retaining wall. Back filling is also done to bring the soil up to final grade.

Brick Ledge: a depression placed in the outside perimeter of a house wherever brick will be located. This depression is created by attaching a two-by-six piece of lumber flat-ways in the side of the foundation exterior vertical form.

Footer: a continuous eight- or ten-inch thick concrete pad that supports the foundation wall or monopost.

Rebar: steel rods put in footings and grade beams in a concrete foundation. They vary in size depending on the structure and what size foundation is being poured.

DOORS

(Exterior Door)

Hiring Contractors

Bored: drilling a specific sized hole for a doorknob or deadbolt.

Brick Mould: a standard type of exterior moulding used on exterior doors. The moulding is thick enough to hide the one-inch air space normally left behind brick.

Dead Bolt: an extra lock that is installed above the normal doorknob. When you buy a door, you can have the door pre-bored for the dead bolt. The deadbolt can be keyed on both sides or just one.

Drip Cap: a piece of flashing usually made out of metal and attached above a door or window. It allows water to drip from the drip cap and not run down the window or door.

Jamb: the framework around the door. The door is connected to the jamb with hinges. Other parts of the jamb of a door are the doorstop and threshold.

Threshold: the device that fills in the gap between the bottom of the door and the finished floor. Some thresholds are adjustable to allow you to create a better seal at the bottom.

(Interior Door)

Door Jamb: the framework where the hinges are attached and the door is hung. The thickness of the doorjamb is an important factor when ordering doors.

Door Stop: a device used to stop the movement of a door in order to prevent damage to something else such as sheetrock.

Door Swing: the way the door opens. This is normally stated as a left hand or a right hand. If you are standing outside a room looking in and the door swings into the room and the hinges are on the left, the door is a left hand door.

Pre-Bored: pre-boring interior or exterior doors for doorknobs at the manufacturing plant. This is easier than trying to bore doors onsite.

Setback: refers to the distance the hole is cut in the door for the doorknob. If the setback is not correct, the doorknob cannot be installed.

Split Jamb: The jamb is split and grooved so it fits and interlocks with the other side.

WINDOWS

Argon Gas: a colorless and odorless gas used to fill the airspace between panes of insulating Low E glass.

Direct Glaze: a window with no sash. The glass is glazed directly into the frame and is stationary. Addition of argon greatly increases the insulating performance of the Low E glass.

Double Hung: a window with two movable sashes that operate vertically. Double hung sash are held in an open position with coil spring block and tackle balancing devices.

Glazing: a method of installing glass into windows and doors.

Insulating Glass: two panes of glass separated by a spacer and hermetically sealed together with dead air space between the panes.

Low E Window: a window with a low emittance coating applied to the surface of the glass. This coating is almost invisible and reflects certain wavelengths or frequencies of sunlight.

Rough Opening: an opening in the wall where a window or door unit is to be installed. Openings are larger than the size of the unit to allow room for insulation and to shim the unit square.

Sash: a portion of the window unit separate from the frame.

Single Hung Window: a window with only one operable sash. In an aluminum window, the only sash that is operable is the bottom sash.

Tempered: glass-heated and then cooled rapidly in a controlled environment. This process makes the glass stronger than regular glass. Tempering also makes the glass safer because when broken it yields small pebble-like fragments.

Tinted Windows: windows with a coating applied that reduces the heat and gives the glass color. The most common colors are amber and gray.

Vinyl Glazing Bead: a vinyl extrusion used on clad units which serves the same purpose as a wood glazing bead for wood units.

Weather-Stripping: a strip of resilient material designed to seal the sash and frame members to reduce air and water infiltration.

Window Balance: a mechanical device that acts as a counterweight to assist in the opening and closing of the windows. In old wood windows, the window balances were weights tied to ropes inside the window jambs.

Window Fin (or Nailing Fin): the metal strip around the perimeter of the window. This strip allows the window to be nailed to the wall sheathing.

Learn Contractor Lingo: Terminology

XO: the letters identify the operation of window or door units as viewed from the exterior. O stands for stationary while X stands for operating.

FLOORING

Baseboard: boards placed against the bottom of walls. Conceals the joint between walls and floors and gives a finished appearance.

Base Shoe: molding used to finish off the bottom edge of the baseboard, and is used to hide irregular floor and wall joints.

Countersink: to drive a nail or screw below the surface.

Drum Sander: a specialized floor sander (about the size of a walk-behind lawn mower) pushed along the floor's open areas.

Filler: wood putty used to patch holes and pores to create a smooth, consistent surface. These fillers are available in various colors to match different types of wood.

Frieze: a carpet style where the yarn is tightly twisted to give it a nubby, rough appearance.

Floating Floor: a floor system that can be placed on top of an existing floor and does not need to be nailed down. Tiles or boards are glued together rather than directly affixed to the sub floor or floor.

Joist: a parallel framing member installed horizontally to carry floor and ceiling loads.

Laminate: thin layers of wood or plastic veneer glued to an inner core.

Parquet Flooring: woodwork floors set in geometric forms for design purposes.

Pickled Floors: an informal, casual look created by rubbing white paint into already stained or finished wood flooring.

Pilot Hole: a pre-drilled hole that makes it possible to drive a screw or nail without splitting wood.

Plywood: a piece of wood made of three or more layers of veneer wood bonded together with glue. For strength, the middle layer is usually placed so the grain runs perpendicular to the layers above and below it.

Prefinished Floor: finished flooring that requires installation only.

Subfloor: boards or plywood mounted over joists on which the finish floor is laid.

Terrazzo: a multi-colored floor made from stone or marble chips embedded in cement.

Underlayment: any material placed over the subfloor to provide a smooth, stable surface for the finish material, such as plywood, particleboard, or foam pad.

Quarter Round: a small-sized molding that has the profile of a quarter circles, frequently used as base molding.

PAINTING

Accelerator: any substance that increases the speed of a chemical reaction. In paint terms, a material that hastens the curing or cross-linking of a resin system.

Learn Contractor Lingo: Terminology

Alligatoring: a scaly pattern that appears on paint due to the inability of the paint to bond to a glossy coating beneath it.

Backer Rod: an extruded foam rod that is normally placed in joints that are deeper than one-half inch, which provides a backing when the joint is caulked.

Bleeding: an underlying substance or material showing through after the area is painted.

Blistering: swollen areas caused by oil or grease under film, water in spray line, or trapped solvent during spraying or transmission of moisture.

Boxing: mixing together of the different cans of similar paint to be used on a job to ensure consistency of color.

Caulking: a generic term for a compound used to fill cracks, gaps, seams, and joints.

Chalking: deterioration of the surface of an exterior paint after weathering. The paint will appear faded and powdery. Chalk should be removed prior to repainting.

Cutting In: painting a surface adjacent to another surface that wasn't meant to be painted. Cutting in is normally done before the painter uses a roller to roll the surface such as a wall.

Latex: dispersion of a solid in a liquid. Often used as a synonym for a dispersion binder.

Primer: a first coat in a paint system whose main function is to provide the adhesion between substrate and the total paint system.

Roller Application: applying coating material by means of a hand-held roller of some soft material, such as foamed plastic, fabric, or wool.

Sealer: a coating whose main functions are to 1) reduce gross porosity or 2) to seal in aggressive chemicals (e.g., alkalinity).

Thinner: a volatile organic liquid used to reduce the viscosity of a coating; often a blend of different solvents and diluents.

Varnish: a transparent coating material based essentially on resins and/or drying oils and solvents.

LIGHTING

Amperes/Amps: a measure of electrical current.

Ballast: an auxiliary piece of equipment required to start and to properly control the flow of current to gas discharge light sources such as fluorescent and high intensity discharge (HID) lamps.

Compact Fluorescent Lamp (CFL): fluorescent lamps that are single-ended and have smaller diameter tubes bent to form a compact shape. Some CFLs have integral ballasts and medium or candelabra screw bases for easy replacement of incandescent lamps.

Luminaire: a complete lighting unit consisting of a lamp and ballast together with the parts designed to distribute the light, to position and protect the lamps, and to connect them to the power supply. A luminaire is often referred to as a fixture.

Sconce: a light fixture attached to a wall.

Voltage: a measurement of the electromotive force in an electrical circuit or device expressed in volts. Voltage can be thought of as being analogous to the pressure in a waterline.

Watt: a unit of electrical power. Lamps are rated in watts to indicate the rate at which they consume energy.

LANDSCAPING

Accent: the use of a plant or object to draw attention to a specific place or area.

Acidic Soil: soil with a PH level of less than 7.0.

Alkaline Soil: soil with a PH level of more than 7.0.

Annual: flowering plants that last only one season.

Arbor: an open framework designed to offer shade and a resting place in a garden. Arbors are often made of rustic wood or latticework that also serves as a trellis on which climbing plants can grow.

Arcade: a series of arches that form a walkway with a ceiling. Most often formed by rows of trees, but can also be formed by other plants or be man-made.

Belvedere: any structure, such as a gazebo or other roofed edifice, that provides a good view of the landscape.

Biennial: plants that grow for one year without flowering then produce flowers or fruits in the second year before dying.

Deciduous: trees and shrubs that shed their leaves or foliage in the fall.

Hiring Contractors

Decking: decks made out of wood or composite materials to create a recreational area.

Edging: use of strong lines of division to accentuate the separation of one area from another in a landscape.

Evergreen: plants that remain green throughout the year.

Ground Cover: plants that grow horizontal to the ground. Ground cover is often the best solution for shady and high traffic areas.

Hardscape: sidewalks, patios, and walkways.

Landscaping Fabric: a synthetic landscaping material that blocks out sun, soil, and weeds but allows water to pass through.

Mulch: a layer of either inorganic or organic material used to control weeds and increase water retention.

Patio: any paved area (concrete, brick, or flagstone) meant for recreational purposes.

Perennial: any flowering plant that returns year after year.

Rotunda: any circular, domed building, often used in landscaping to create a shaded area suitable for rest and relaxation.

Stacking: supporting a tree, to hold it in place, using ropes or wooden stacks.

Terracing: building walls to hold the soil in place on a sloped landscape.

Topiary: a garden where plants or shrubs are shaped and trimmed into geometric or animal forms.

Xeriscape: landscaping designed specifically for areas that are susceptible to drought or for areas where water conservation is practiced.

HOME DECOR

Accessories: small objects such as vases, books, lamps, plants and florals, and sculptures used to adorn and personalize a room.

Antiquing: a process in which an object or surface is intentionally distressed or discolored to provide the appearance of age.

Armoire: a large wardrobe or movable closet for storing clothing; often also used to hide televisions, audio/video equipment, or computer workstations.

Bergere Chair: a large armchair usually associated with the French Country or Provençale decorating style. It often features an upholstered seat, back, and arms, a loose seat cushion, and an exposed wooden frame.

Beveled Glass: clear or mirrored glass in which the edge perimeter (usually one-inch wide) has been cut at an angle for a contrasting visual effect. On clear glass, it creates a distorted prism effect, and on mirrored glass it adds a reflective "sparkle".

Blinds: rigid or soft window coverings, oriented either horizontally or vertically, that obscure light, provide privacy, and can be raised, lowered, or adjusted to different levels.

Camelback Sofa: a type of sofa with a curved back, typically seen in more traditional styles, such as Queen Anne, Chippendale, or Federal.

Chair Rail: a piece of decorative molding placed approximately thirty inches off the floor to protect walls from being scraped by chair backs.

Chaise Lounge: a long, low upholstered couch in the shape of a chair that is long enough to support the legs.

Commode: a stand or cupboard traditionally used for storing chamber pots. Often used as a side table or nightstand.

Console Table: a long narrow table used for displaying decorative objects, lighting, or flowers, and is often placed in a foyer or behind a sofa.

Contemporary: the style inherent to the present time, often confused with "modern."

Credenza: a large low cabinet, usually thirty to thirty-six inches high with a flat top used for serving and storage.

Curtain Panel: a large piece of fabric designed to cover part or all of a window, usually hung in pairs.

Étagère: a small, upright set of freestanding open-sided shelves used for displaying small decorative items.

Faux-finish: a decorative technique in which paint or stain is applied to a surface to simulate another material such as wood, marble, or granite.

Finial: a decorative end piece on a curtain rod, often in the shape of a spear, ball, leaf, or pineapple.

Focal point: a visual center of interest or point of emphasis in a room. A well-designed room will have many engaging focal points.

Futon: a Japanese-style mattress that is placed on the floor or on a folding wooden or metal frame. Used as both a seating place and bed.

Grommet: an eyelet in a piece of fabric reinforced with two pieces of affixed metal. Often found on contemporary curtain panels.

Learn Contractor Lingo: Terminology

Highboy: a tall, narrow chest of drawers usually placed in bedrooms.

Knife-Edge: a sewing technique found on decorative cushions that uses a single seam or welt around a cushion's perimeter.

Mid-Century Modern: a decorative style first popularized in the late 1940s characterized by clean lines, the use of modern materials such as plastic and aluminum, and a sleek, minimal profile. The style reached its apex in the late 1950s and early 1960s, but continued to be popular into the early 1970s. In the past few years, the style has enjoyed resurgence in popularity with several books, websites, and contemporary knockoffs.

Mullion: wood or metal dividers used between the different panes of glass on multi-paned windows. Modern windows often feature faux decorative mullions.

Objet d'Art: a small object of artistic value often used as a decorative element.

Ottoman: an upholstered stool or hassock, designed to go at the foot of a chair. Often used in contemporary interiors in place of a coffee table.

Platform Bed: a low, self-contained bed frame that features slats or webbing for suspension eliminating the need for a box spring.

Primary Colors: the three basic colors of which all other colors are comprised of: red, yellow, and blue.

Runner: a long, narrow area rug designed to go in a hallway or foyer.

Sconce: a wall-mounted light fixture.

Sectional Furniture: modular furniture, usually seating pieces, which can be combined into different combinations.

Settee: a long wooden or upholstered bench with a back. Designed to seat two or more people.

Shade: any color mixed with black. Most rich, ultra-dark colors are shades.

Sideboard: a long storage chest often used for serving and storage in a formal dining room.

Sisal: strong fiber from the leaves of the sisal plant used to create area rugs and broadloom floor coverings.

Slipcover: a removable fabric cover for a chair, sofa, or loveseat, and can be either custom-tailored or adjusted with ties and fasteners.

Table Runner: a long, narrow, decorative strip of fabric running down the middle of a table.

Task lighting: a lighting source directed to a specific area within a room for a specific purpose. Reading lights in a living room or under-counter lighting in a kitchen are examples of task lighting.

Throw Pillow: a small square or round decorative pillow usually found on sofas, chairs, or beds.

Upholstery: the process of fitting furniture, usually seating, that has padding, springs, and webbing, with a fabric or leather cover.

Vintage: furniture and decorative elements that are between ten and 100 years old. Often found at flea markets, garage sales, and specialty vintage retailers.

MISCELLANEOUS

Chalk Line: a useful tool for marking a straight line. Features a line that is

Learn Contractor Lingo: Terminology

reeled out from a chalk-filled canister, hooked at one end of the intended cut line, tensioned, and snapped.

Hammer Drill: specially designed tool to both rotate a bit and apply a pulsing pressure that breaks through masonry neatly, faster, and more easily than with rotary action alone. Intended for concrete and other masonry work.

Integral Sink: sink made from the same material as the countertop to form a continuous surface.

Paver Tile: a tile that is larger than six square inches.

Pyrolave: countertop material made from enameled lava rock.

Retrofit: upgrading a preexisting fixture by installing new parts.

Shim: a thin piece of wood used during installation to ensure that countertops are level.

Substrate: any surface to which a paint, stain, or sealant is applied.

Square: a tool equipped with a six-inch steel rule for marking ninety-degree and forty-five-degree angles.

Tongue and Groove: a way of connecting materials, such as wood, in which the tongue of a board is placed into the groove of the board following it.

Veneer: a thin piece of wood attached to particleboard to create the illusion of wood surfaces.

Volatile Organic Compounds (VOCs): materials that evaporate from organic products and can cause acute and chronic illnesses.

Wood Shakes: rough, thick, uneven shingles, either hand split or sawed, that can be used as siding material.

About the Authors

Steven R. VanCauwenbergh is a long-time investor in income-producing properties and has mastered the critical areas of purchasing, financing, renovating and managing real estate. He has authored several books and courses empowering people to reach their goals of financial freedom. He is a highly sought after personal coach and teaches his techniques in seminars across the country.

Walter B. Jenkins is the proud father of international hockey sensation Katie Jenkins. Before beginning his career as a writer and speaker, Walter was an attorney and sports agent. He now helps people turn their ideas into great books. In his spare time he enjoys studying tae kwon do, scuba diving, riding his bike, and training his German shepherd, Jake the wonder dog. Learn more at www.walterbjenkins.com.

Many Thanks!

I would like to thank everyone who has contributed to this project, Walter B. Jenkins for his grace and leadership, Elizabeth Hunt art direction, Jason Grotelueschen input, Miranda Moore edits, Heather Schleeper proof reading, Dean Wendt the voice, John Day to GO BIGGER! This book would not be a reality if it wasn't for my loving family and their encouragement, my dear wife Shannez' and my mother Linda for being by my side through the entire process.

I would like to thank all the interviewees for giving me their time and wisdom.

Friends I appreciate:

Devin Long
Steven Earp
Greg Brister
Ken & Sharlene Monier
Zac McDorr
Ben Shrewsbury
Ed O'Toole
Scott Smith
Bryon Hanawalt
Donny Ho
Dutch Revenboer
Kenny Malabag
Linda Hamilton
Pam Schrader
Bille Presnell

Delton Brown
Alvin Smith
Raymond Moya
Jacquith Farris
Stephen King
Brandon Bull
Masie Bross
Justin McGavock
Shawn McVicker
Alex Albers
Robert Elder
Dan McCown
Jeffery Taylor

Don't have the time to read?
Listen!

Audiobook Now Available:

You will hear real life examples of real estate investment issues and how to deal with them.

301 AUDIO TRACKS, 3+ HOURS OF MATERIAL

MAXIMIZE YOUR LEARNING CURVE

Get your copy today at www.thesavvylandlordbook.com

Interested in learning more?

CALL NOW
405-633-1008

• *one-on-one coaching available*

NEW BOOK FROM THE SAVVY LANDLORD

301 Questions with Real Answers!

For Every Real Estate Investor & Landlord

If you are a new or seasoned investor this book is for you!

Learn more, plus save time and money!

Real Estate is a long term investment. How can I make money right now?
I have prospective tenant with a felony conviction. Should I rent to them?
How do I analyze a property and know it's going to cash flow?
What is title insurance?
My tenant claims to be a handyman. Should I have him work off this rent?
Do I have to have an attorney represent me when filing an eviction?
The tenant wants to buy the property. How does "rent to own" work?
What does PMI mean?
How do I protect myself from being sued by my tenant?
What is a materialmen's lien?
and 291 more questions that will be answered!

Additional Bonus Section of 20+ Tips!

Get your copy today at thesavvylandlordbook.com

Don't have the time to read?
Listen!

Audiobook Now Available:

You will hear real life examples of real estate investment issues and how to deal with them.

20+ AUDIO TRACKS, 3+ HOURS OF MATERIAL

MAXIMIZE YOUR LEARNING CURVE

Get your copy today at www.thesavvylandlordbook.com

CONNECT AT:
thesavvylandlordbook.com

Freebies

Down-loadable Forms

New Products

Tips

Blog

Twitter: twitter.com/landlordbook
Facebook: facebook.com/thesavvylandlord
Email: info@thesavvylandlordbook.com

■ ■ ■

Portion of the proceeds will benefit Whiz Kids

The mission of Whiz Kids is to improve the well-being of inner-city youth through academic tutoring and positive mentoring relationships.

About Whiz Kids

Founded in 1996, under the umbrella of the 501(c) 3 nonprofit, City Care, Inc., Whiz Kids is a nonprofit, one-on-one, tutoring and mentoring program for at-risk students in the Oklahoma City metropolitan area. Whiz Kids collaboratively and creatively addresses Oklahoma City's urban social and educational crisis by matching tutor/mentors with at-risk students. Teachers select students for the Whiz Kids program because they are reading below their grade level and can benefit from a mentoring relationship. Tutors are paired with a child and meet weekly with the same child during the school year for a one-on-one after-school tutoring session. Whiz Kids sites are churches in each school's community that donate their facility and provide tutors and on-site coordinators. These urban churches are partnered with other metro area (typically suburban) churches to provide additional volunteers and tutors, essentially bringing the resource of people back to the urban neighborhoods where the children live. Each site has a liaison teacher from the school that serves as an educational consultant, and is a resource for the volunteer tutors.

In order to qualify for the Whiz Kids program, a school must have at least 87% of its students eligible for free/reduced lunch. Seventeen of the Whiz Kids schools have percentages higher than 95% free/reduced lunch and four are 100% free/reduced lunch. Because of this, Whiz Kids serves children who live in some of Oklahoma City's most desperate neighborhoods, where poverty, illiteracy and violence often strangle a child's promise. The schools served by the Whiz Kids program are mostly Oklahoma City Public Schools, but also include a few schools in the Crooked Oak, Putnam City, Mid-Del and Crutcho districts.

Since its inception, one school and a handful of volunteers, Whiz Kids has grown to serve more than 800 students from 29 at-risk elementary schools, in partnership with 63 churches.

Get involved and make an impact!

www.whizkidsok.org

www.savvyinvestors.com

www.ingramcontent.com/pod-product-compliance
Lightning Source LLC
Chambersburg PA
CBHW071705090426
42738CB00009B/1667